Trees and Woodlands in Cheshire

A History and Guide

Richard Smart

Cheshire Landscape Trust

This edition published in Great Britain by
Cheshire Landscape Trust
10 Elizabeth Crescent
Queens Park
Chester
CH4 7AZ

ISBN 0-9520342-0-4

CIP details for this book are available from the British Library

Typeset and designed by
Bridge Books, Wrexham, Clwyd

Printed and bound by WBC Ltd, Bridgend, Mid Glamorgan

Contents

The Cheshire Landscape Trust acknowledge and thank the following sponsors for their assistance in the production of this book:-

ICI Chemical & Polymers Ltd

The Bolesworth Estate Co
The Capesthorne Estate
Cheshire County Council
Viscount Cholmondeley
The Earl of Derby's Estates
The Duchy of Lancaster
S Z Ferranti Esq
The Grosvenor Estate
National Westminster Bank, Chester
Pilkington plc
Shotton Paper Co plc
Vauxhall Motors Ltd
The Wellcome Foundation
Sir Richard Baker Wilbraham

Foreword

By His Grace The Duke of Westminster

Eaton Hall · Chester

Cheshire faces many challenges in the years ahead. The need to protect and conserve valuable features in the landscape has never been greater.

Cheshire is a county with a long woodland tradition. Trees have always played a significant role in the County's landscape, economy and way of life. Yet with only 4% of the County currently given over to trees and woods, it is markedly less well endowed than other counties, and significantly below the national average of 10%.

Trees and woodlands are a renewable resource, capable of responding to the changing demands and needs of an informed, concerned and mobile population, seeking both recreation and an attractive environment both for its own benefit and also for wildlife. Viable woodlands provide the raw materials and can help revive some traditional country crafts, with the potential for job creation in rural communities.

Richard Smart, a professional forester and land manager has done an excellent job in researching and writing a book which celebrates the past and looks forward to the future of Cheshire's trees and woodland.

As President of the Cheshire Landscape Trust and a lover of trees I welcome the publication of this book. I hope that it will inspire men, women and children in the County to care for our woodland heritage by thinking globally and acting locally.

INTRODUCTION

As a practising consultant forester I have been involved with trees and woodlands in Cheshire for almost twenty years, but my interest in woodland history was first stirred some ten years ago by Dr Graeme White who conducts the excellent Landscape History Diploma courses at Chester College with such enthusiasm.

Cheshire's 1981-2 Year of the Environment and a grant from the County Council's Seedcorn Fund together with very generous support from woodland owners and industry, provided the opportunity to research past records of estate woodlands and forests and piece fragments of information together into a history. Inevitably there are gaps remaining to be filled, for records prior to the 18th century are very scarce indeed.

It is hoped that the chapter on notable trees in the county is a start towards compiling a Cheshire register of historic and exceptional trees. Many species are not included in the list while there are certain to be some omissions in those that are described. Do please write to the Cheshire Landscape Trust at Fountains Building, Upper Northgate Street, Chester CH1 4EF about them.

Some of the notable trees are growing in parks, estates, and gardens on private land, which may only be open to the public at particular times. Unless they are visited when open, which in some cases only occurs once or twice during the summer, if at all, permission to visit should be obtained from the owner.

In the records early names of trees can be confusing. Balsam of Guilead which occurs frequently in the first conifer plantings is one of the silver firs, *Abies balsamea*. The Norway spruce, *Picea abies*, was referred to as Spruce fir. The native Scots pine, *Pinus sylvestris*, was variously referred to as Scots, Scotch, Scotch fir, and fir in early records. In many cases I have changed the latter names to Scots pine in the text.

At an early stage the Cheshire Landscape Trust gave their support to the project. John Gittins, their Director, has been a constant source of encouragement as has the County Forestry Officer, Robert Price who has helped throughout providing leads and suggestions and finally, together with his staff, checking parts of the text. In the latter connection I also have to thank Peter Legard and Oliver Bott, both making helpful suggestions.

Libraries and their staff have always been cheerful and most helpful, particularly the County Records Office and Chester City Records Office who have borne the brunt of the enquiries, but also the Boat Museum, Merseyside Maritime Records

Centre, John Rylands University Library of Manchester, Royal Forestry Society Library in Tring, Forest Authority Library at Alice Holt Research Station, the RSA Library in London, and the Public Records Office in Kew.

The Salt Museum in Northwich together with Mr D G Twigg, and the Pilkington Glass Museum in St Helens together with Mrs R H Vose, provided much information on the use of wood in the salt and glass industry respectively.

Mr C F Foster's help in extracting woodland records from the Arley Estate Archives was invaluable, as was Mr C J Henratty's assistance with Capesthorne and Tabley Estate Records. I am also indebted to Mr A F Mitchell and Mr J K Hulme for information on notable trees. Considerable assistance was received from many others including:- Mr L Adams, Mr P Attfield, Mr and Mrs D Bailey, Mr A G Barbour, Dr R A Benton, Mr E Broadbent, The Marchioness of Cholmondeley, Mr F Crewe, Mr M Emmerson, Mr J Gibbs, Mr B Goulden, Mr M A O Hedley, Mr C F Legh, The Countess of Lindsay, Sir Bernard Lovell, Dr H McAllister, Mr G McGowan, Mr A C Miller, Mr G S Ridley, Mr R G Scaife, Mr G Stockton, Mr P Sharples, Mr D Wainwright, Mr K Williams of Macclesfield, the Tree Register of the British Isles, and many Council and Estate staff.

To all the above and others who have helped, my sincere thanks.

Richard Smart
Chester
1992

CHAPTER 1 - The Landscape Background

Most of Cheshire is low lying plain under 100m in altitude, formed by post glacial deposits of sands, gravels and clays of rocks of the triassic period. In the east the plain is edged by the millstone grits and shales of the Pennines which rise to the highest point in the county at Shining Tor, 559m. In the centre, the plain is broken by the sandstone ridge which extends from Runcorn in the north through Helsby and along the Bickerton Hills rising to 227m at Rawhead, and further east by the smaller but equally attractive outlying ridge with a steep scarp on the north east side, Alderley Edge.

The post glacial deposits vary from boulder clay that gives rise to the heavy soils which support Cheshire's dairy farms, to sand deposits with light acidic soils. The latter are more suited to horticulture, forestry and mineral working than farming, and occur particularly in the Delamere, Rudheath, and Congleton areas.

Incisions have been made through the post glacial deposits by the rivers Bollin, Dane, Weaver and their tributaries, in places exposing the underlying bedrock and creating small narrow-sided valleys. There are some delightful local landscapes here, sometimes enhanced by small semi-natural woods perched on the valley side with a rich ground flora.

Other features of the county are the meres formed in hollows in undulating moraine, such as Redesmere, often with associated alder on the fringe, and the mosses where hollows are filled with sphagnum, such as Wybunbury and Abbotts Moss. There are also limited areas of raised peatmoss occurring on the level sites such as Dane and Lindow Moss.

On the Pennine edge in the east the cloughs feeding the Dane, Goyt, and Etherow cut deeply into the hillside forming a fine landscape. This was part of the ancient Macclesfield Forest but only a few remnants of semi natural woodland remain, mainly on steep hillsides where oak is the dominant tree species. The grits and the shales of the carboniferous age are often exposed on the surface, while limited coal deposits occur.

The annual rainfall varies from approximately 800mm on the western edge of the county to 1000mm on the lower Pennine slopes in the east.

Less than 4% of Cheshire is currently woodland against a national average of 10%, yet the county has the appearance of being comparatively well wooded for many hedgerow trees have been retained, even if in some cases the hedgerow itself has been removed. Approximately 74% of the woodland consists mainly of broadleaved trees, though there is often a coniferous element. There are some extensive blocks of woodland but the majority of the woods are quite small in area and dispersed as might be expected in a predominantly agricultural county.

These, together with the pattern of fields, the hedgerows and hedgerow trees are the essence of the rural landscape in the county, further enhanced by the parks and estates with fine historic landscapes created by design rather than by a long gradual process of change.

The two great rivers, the Mersey which marks much of the northern boundary of the county, and the Dee which forms part of the western boundary, are important features for they have had a great influence on settlement and development over the centuries.

There have been several changes to the boundaries of the county during the last century, but its present area is 232,846 hectares. For the purposes of this book the county includes all that is and has been Cheshire.

Chapter 2 - The Ancient Woodland

When the ice retreated around 12,000 years ago, forests of birch, aspen, willow and some juniper started to colonise the tundra. These were followed by pine and hazel, then wych elm, oak, and other species coming in from northern Europe, which was still linked to Britain as the climate started to warm. The word 'wildwood' has been used to describe this forest, which, within a few thousand years covered the country.

The whole of Cheshire, including the Pennine uplands, was almost certainly clothed in forest by 5000 BC when birch and pine, with some hazel and oak, were the main species. With further climatic change in the boreal and Atlantic periods there were changes in the species in the forest with pine receding and alder increasing. At the same time oak was becoming more dominant in a mixed deciduous forest.

During the warm and wet Atlantic period around 4000 BC, mixed deciduous forest dominated by oak prevailed, and trees such as the small leaved lime and wych elm were common, particularly at the lower levels. Pollen analysis has shown a marked decline in the elm population since 3000 BC. The date of entry of ash as a major component of wet deciduous woodland sites is uncertain, though probably relatively recent. Ash charcoal has been found on eleven sites dated as neolithic or later in Wales, while some pollen is present in the sub-boreal period [1]. The decline in the elm population may have been due to man's influence for it is a particularly suitable tree for leaf fodder for pounded stock and trees may have been felled and lopped to provide it [2]. As lime and ash are also suitable fodder trees and still used as such on parts of the continent such as the south of France, they could have been similarly affected, though some attribute the reduction of lime to the deliberate grubbing out of lime woods [3].

In historic times oak had remained the principal dominant tree in Cheshire. Sessile oak, *Quercus petraea,* is found in the uplands, on the sandstone ridges, and on the light acidic sandy soils. Pedunculate oak, *Quercus robur,* is generally found on the heavier soils in the Cheshire plain.

In 1465, Sir Peter Legh described some trees at Lyme Park and mentioned that the following kinds were growing on the estate:- alder, birch, willow, oak, aspen, elder, thorn, bramble, rose, woodrose, holly, blackberry, crab, cherry, broomheath, and arbutus [4]. All these are native species. There is no mention of beech now such a feature of many of the woods at Lyme. This tree is not native to Cheshire. It was not introduced into the county until about 1650 when Thomas Stanley at Alderley obtained some beechmast from Kyre, Worcestershire.

There are thirty-three native tree species in Britain [5] and of these beech and hornbeam were confined to southern Britain and South Wales, and Scots pine was confined to Scotland. Pine will only regenerate from seed and this, together with its ready destruction by fire and susceptibility to grazing by both farmstock and wildlife, almost certainly accounts for its disappearance as a native tree in Cheshire and other English and Welsh counties.

Common hardwoods which are not part of the wildwood are the English elm, sweet chestnut, horse chestnut, and sycamore, all of which were introduced into the country.

Almost all the native species are able to regenerate from coppice shoots from the stump when they are felled. The wild cherry and poplars are exceptions but they regenerate from root suckers. It is the great resilience of our native hardwoods which has enabled the wildwood to regenerate and, in a few cases, to continue to this day as a relic of ancient woodland.

Besides cultivation there have been many factors influencing our wildwood over the ages. The shifting cultivation carried out by neolithic farmers was normally accompanied by burning branchwood in order to improve the fertility of the soil, a system still used in parts of Africa today. Fire was the cause of much damage to the wildwood from early times, but a far greater influence particularly on upland sites, has been continuous grazing which led to grassland replacing many woodland areas.

This was one of the main factors in the uplands of Macclesfield Forest where grassland predominated when it became royal forest around the time of Domesday. Here, as in the other royal forests, grazing continued to be important for both deer and husbanded livestock.

Initially there was more emphasis on the deer as hunting was the reason for creating the forest. Some grassland areas could have reverted to woodland, but again at a later date this secondary woodland could have been returned to farming as pressure on the forest increased.

Succession from pasture or arable land to oak woodland can be comparatively quick in some cases, particularly on good quality land with Pedunculate oak on the lowland loams and clays [6]. There is little knowledge of the speed of succession of the sessile oak, but it is likely to behave in a similar way if grazing by stock and rabbits is excluded.

Ancient woodlands have been defined by the Nature Conservancy Council as being sites continuously wooded since 1600, composed of relatively natural stands of native species. There are probably no truly natural stands in existence in Cheshire for every woodland must surely have been affected by man directly or indirectly, so it is more correct to describe these woods as semi-natural.

These woodlands are not always easy to identify. They may exist as high forest, coppice which is rare in Cheshire, or possibly recently felled woodland having the appearance of scrub. Mature plantations made up of mostly native species growing where they would normally grow naturally, may look very like natural woodland, particularly if oak dominates for the ground flora and shrub layer may be substantially the same. From the late 18th century it was almost standard practice to plant oak with conifer nurses which were removed as the oak matured. Within a few years there is no trace of the conifer stumps which have rotted away.

There are a number of indicators which can be used to identify ancient woodland sites. One of these is the shape of the woodland, for they have characteristically irregular boundaries.

Rackham recognised two main types, sinuous shapes which are a series of curves and zigzag shapes with abrupt changes in direction. These are in contrast to the straight line boundaries or regular curves of recent woodlands. Another possible indication is the marking of boundaries by massive banks and ditches which would follow an irregular boundary, while sometimes changes of level are found where woodlands adjoin arable land, often known as lynchets [7].

An indicator of secondary woodland, that is woodland which for a time was under agriculture, is the presence of old ridge and furrow showing as regular undulations in the ground surface. This is noticeable in some of the small sporting coverts on the Cheshire plain. Place names can also give some indication and should always be examined though they can also mislead. If the wood is called a covert, gorse, heath, moss, or plantation it can be assumed that it is not ancient.

Plants can also be used as indicators of sites of ancient woodland, but most work on these indicators has been researched in eastern and southern England. Rackham cites the herb Paris, *Paris quadrifolia*, oxslip, *Primula elatior*, woodland hawthorn, *Crataegus laevigata*, and wild service tree, *Sorbus torminalis,* as being almost entirely confined to ancient woodland in East Anglia, but suggests that evidence from indicator plants should be based on their behaviour locally rather than nationally [8].

Another authority, Peterken, lists five plants which appear to be mainly restricted to ancient woodland throughout their British range as:- lily of the valley, *Convallaria majalis*, hay scented buckler fern, *Dryopteris aemula*, oxslip, wild service tree, and small leaved lime, *Tilia cordata* [9]. All these species occur in Cheshire with the exception of the hay scented buckler fern, but the lily of the valley may be naturalised and is not part of any particular community [10].

The Cheshire suite of indicators should include herb paris, oxslip, wild service tree, and small leaved lime, to which alder buckthorn, *Frangula alnus*, spindle, *Euonymus europaeus*, and field maple, *Acer campestre*, might be added. The service tree is evident in woods in the Weaver valley, Darnhall, and Shotwick areas, while large field maple are found in the Acton Bridge and Audlem area.

In an agricultural county like Cheshire, ancient woodlands are mainly found either along streams or valleys which are wet or steeply sided so that they are difficult to farm or graze, along edges or outliers of estates parishes or townships in areas most remote from central activity, and in areas where access is difficult and ground conditions such that harvesting is impracticable.

The surest way to identify ancient sites is to find early written or drawn evidence from old maps, charters, estate records, and other documents.

The Nature Conservancy Council, or English Nature as it is called now, produced a preliminary inventory of ancient woodland in Cheshire in 1988 based largely on a desk survey using first edition ordnance survey maps, air photographs, and existing woodland descriptions to hand. This has provisionally identified sites of ancient woodland together with the areas of plantation and semi-natural ancient woodland within them, a valuable first step towards their conservation. As their inventory report states in the foreword, more detailed studies of the woods need to be carried out, particularly on the many small ancient woods in the county, before they can be certain of the exact extent of ancient woodland and its present state. However the survey in Cheshire was undertaken with considerable care and it is unlikely that the total figures of 1687 hectares of ancient woodland sites, made up of 1263 hectares of semi-natural ancient woodland and 424 hectares of plantation, will change appreciably [11].

The 1263 hectares of ancient woodland with its associated flora rich habitats supporting a wide range of wildlife, is a priceless asset and every effort should be made to conserve it. Woodland conservation requires sympathetic management so that the essential long term structure of the community is maintained. Nature does not stand still. From time to time some felling and regeneration is necessary is addition to regular maintenance. The Forest Authority has made special provision for these woodlands in the Woodland Grant Scheme. Both the Authority and the County Forestry Officer hold copies of the Ancient Woodland Provisional Inventory. They can also give general advice on the provisions of the Woodland Grant Scheme.

The area of ancient woodland sites has declined by 6% in Cheshire between 1920 and 1988 when the Nature Conservancy Council carried out their survey. Now we know its extent, status, and value, we all have a responsibility to ensure there is no further decline. Sixty-three per cent of the ancient woodland area is made up of small woods under 5 hectares in extent. Added protection would be provided if buffer zones of similar species were planted around them, while in some cases it may be possible to link adjacent small woods. Consideration should be given to providing an incentive to woodland owners to create buffer zones, possibly in the form of a fencing grant.

CHAPTER 3 - Sources of Historical Information on Woodland

Peat

Peat bogs and mosses were estimated to cover 18,000 acres of Cheshire in 1808, but they had been much more extensive. Areas had been reduced by exploitation for fuel in the 17th and 18th centuries, drainage, and subsequent agricultural development. These processes have continued but fortunately there are still many wetland areas remaining though often quite small in extent. Studies of the peat can yield much information on our past and environmental history.

Peat has formed in large layers over the centuries and wooden articles such as the iron age logboats from Baddiley and Cholmondeley Meres, bodies such as the Lindow man, pollen grains, tree stumps and logs, charcoal and other items can be preserved intact and undisturbed. Peat layers can be dated by radiocarbon testing and the pollen within them analysed and identified, so giving indications of vegetational change, forest clearances, and crops.

Currently a team from the Environmental Research Unit, Keele University, is studying White Moss, Alsager, where there are the remains of a prehistoric forest preserved in the peat. Analysis suggests that this part of Cheshire was dominated by pine in the early post glacial period, followed by oak, elm, and possibly lime in the area surrounding the bog, with pine persisting on the edges. Tree stumps are being dated by a combination of dendrochronology, which compares patterns of rings of known date and cross matches them rather like matching finger prints, and radio carbon dating [1].

Research studies at White Moss and elsewhere, together with evidence from previous investigations, are helping to build up more detailed knowledge of the county's environmental history.

To date the earliest evidence of cereal growing has been found at Lindow where wheat and barley type pollen analysed was dated 550 BC, while pollen evidence at Peckforton Mere showed rye type cereal from about the same period. Evidence of significant human activity well before this period was found at Lindow Moss, and at Danes Moss, Risley Moss, Wybunbury Moss, and Hatchmere for there were falls in tree pollens and increases in grass, bracken, weed, and shrub pollen indicating a period of clearance and pastoral land use. The Hatchmere clearance began with elm decline dated as 3319 BC and continued intermittently to 2743 BC [2].

Agricultural activity increased considerably from around 500 BC onwards when there was considerable forest clearance. Mosses were not favoured sites for occupation. More attractive were the areas of lighter soils where the forest was not dense and comparatively easy to clear, and the river valleys.

Domesday

The Domesday survey was carried out in 1086, just twenty years after Duke William of Normandy conquered England. Commissioners were despatched to all parts of the land and amongst their brief was a directive to find out how much woodland there was. It was recorded by area under every village where woodland occurs in each hundred of the country.

Woodlands were recorded by their dimensions, usually given in leagues, together with a note of enclosures or hawks eyries. A league is approximately 1 1/2 miles. For instance, Adlington in Macclesfield Hundred contained woodland 11 leagues long and 2 wide, with 7 enclosures and 4 hawks eyries, but sometimes the measurement was confusing. Knutsford is recorded as containing woodland 1/2 a league long and 2 acres wide. Plainly the measurements are very approximate and can only give an indication of size. [3]

It can be assumed that if woodland was recorded it was present, for all the information was cross checked, but in some cases a number of separate woods could have been blocked together, for in no village is more than one wood recorded. It is possible that some woods could have been missed. Cheshire could be considered to be well wooded for it has been estimated that 27% of the land area of the county was woodland at the time of Domesday [4]. The Wirral was an exception being more intensively cultivated and comparatively lacking in woodland.

There were also considerable areas of waste, that is arable which has gone out of production, some of which might revert back to woodland. These included areas which had been devastated by the Normans in 1070, and possibly some areas that were vacated because of earlier Welsh raiding.

The royal forests are not mentioned by name in Domesday Cheshire though they were appropriated by the crown at about this time. There are however references to the Earl's forest, as for instance under Done and Aldredelie in Eddisbury North Hundred, where it is recorded that it was waste and is now the Earl's forest [5].

Maps

Christopher Saxton produced the first county atlas of England and Wales in Elizabethan times. The Cheshire map, scale nearly 2 3/4 miles to the inch, is dated 1577. No woodland is mapped in though some parks are shown. Trees are represented by a symbol and only when they are drawn in groups is there any indication of areas containing woodland. The Wirral is noticeable for its lack of tree symbols except in the few parks such as Shotwick, Hooton, Puddington and Bidston.

John Speed, who was born in Farndon in 1552, produced his atlas in 1611 but his county map was largely based on Saxton's work and contained little new information as far as woodlands were concerned. The scale is just under three miles to the inch.

The Dutch publishing houses of Blaeu and Jaanson produced county atlases including Cheshire in 1645 and 1646 respectively. They were very similar maps, elegantly drawn. The wooded areas are more clearly defined but still give no boundaries except for parks.

In 1777 Peter Burdett produced a 1 inch to the mile map of Cheshire which was a major advance for the survey was based on triangulation, while the map clearly showed areas of heath, marsh, moss, and common which had not been reclaimed or improved. Unfortunately, the woodlands are not so clearly defined but the map still gives a much better indication of their location than those of previous cartographers. For example, at Adlington the map shows wooded areas southeast, south, and north northwest of the Hall which correspond approximately to Wych Wood, the Wilderness, and Isles Wood.

Trees are represented on Burdett's map as the traditional round crowned hardwood with short bole and its shadow. At Dunham Massey a piece of woodland to the north of Charcoal Road and west of what is now the A556 in the New Park area is shown with a different tree symbol looking very like a conifer. Conifers were planted in some numbers at Dunham around 1750 and this may be the area showing up on Burdett's plan in 1777.

The three Adlington woods are more clearly shown on Greenwood's 1819 1 inch to the mile county map, Swire and Hutching's 1828/9 ¾ inch to the mile, and Bryant's 1829/31 1¼ inch to the mile maps. All these county maps are worth studying for their woodland information.

Between 1833 and 1843 the first edition ordnance survey 1 inch to the mile sheets were produced, but they provide very little additional information and some woodland areas were missed. However at the same time tithe maps were being produced for each township throughout the county, together with a register of tithe apportionments.

The Tithe maps and apportionments provide an almost county wide record of land use at the time, not quite complete for there are occasional gaps due to prior settlement. Most of the maps are dated in the period 1840-50. They provide a much more accurate record of woods, areas, and ownership. The names of many woods are given together with a description as to whether it is woodland, plantation, and occasionally coppice.

During the 1850s the Ordnance Survey started work on the first 25 inch plans, which eventually covered the whole of the county. They were first issued as parish maps with areas outside the parish left blank. From then on the county has been well served by the standard scale ordnance survey sheets.

Much valuable information on woodland history can be found in the many estate plans, and sometimes birds eye views, which were commissioned by estate owners in Cheshire. Landowners needed plans and registers to provide an efficient method of fixing and collecting rents from the many tenants on their estates. Eighteenth century estate plans cover a considerable area of the county for most estates then were considerably larger than they are today.

Arley Estate was mapped in 1744, surveyor unknown, and again in 1790 by George Holland of Middlewich. There is a 1792 field register to go with the Holland map. There are also maps of lands at Sutton drawn in 1754, and lands in Appleton drawn in 1760, surveyors unknown. Both are excellent plans covering large tracts of countryside which were also in Sir Peter Warburton's ownership at the time. Besides showing wooded areas and coppices or copys, there is interesting detail to pick up such as the Appleton Thorn on the 1760 map of Appleton, and a timber yard on the River Weaver just west of the Frodsham Bridge on the 1754 Sutton map [6].

Estate plans are particularly useful if a number were prepared over the years, such as was the case at Tatton Park. Maps were made by John Hussey in 1733, William Emes in 1768, John Earle in 1787, Humphrey Repton in 1791 and Thomas Greave in 1855. Changes in the woodland and landscape features can be followed over a considerable period.

Edward Glanvill and John Walmesley's maps of the Cholmondeley Estate 1726/1734 show the Great Park with a central rond and radiating rides with the park marked mainly planted[7], but it had been absorbed into farmland and woodland by the time Charles White produced his massive plan of the estate in 1781. There is an earlier map of Cholmondeley Park dated 1689, and a plan of the formal garden designed and laid out by George London is included in *Vitruvius Britannicus III*, 1725.

The Grosvenors' commissioned Thomas Badeslade to produce plans of their lands and a series of maps were produced at scales varying from 3 to 6 chains to the inch in 1737-8, together with a general map of *Possessions Of Inheritance of Sir Robert Grosvenor Bart.* Badeslade was an engineer and surveyor who practiced nationally, and he is best known for the minature atlas of all the English and Welsh counties that he produced in 1841 in conjunction with W H Toms. In the 19th century the estate used locally based surveyors John Davis of Mollington from 1834-47, W Worrall of Chester in 1848, and John Allen Jnr of the Corn Exchange, Chester in 1864-6.

Bolesworth Estate was mapped by G M Elliot of Regent Street, London in 1826 and Capesthorne Estate by J Dunn of Hertford in 1827. Standards were high by the 19th century and maps themselves were often works of art and beautifully drawn. Elliot's maps of Bolesworth Estate are a fine example of the standard of workmanship to be found.

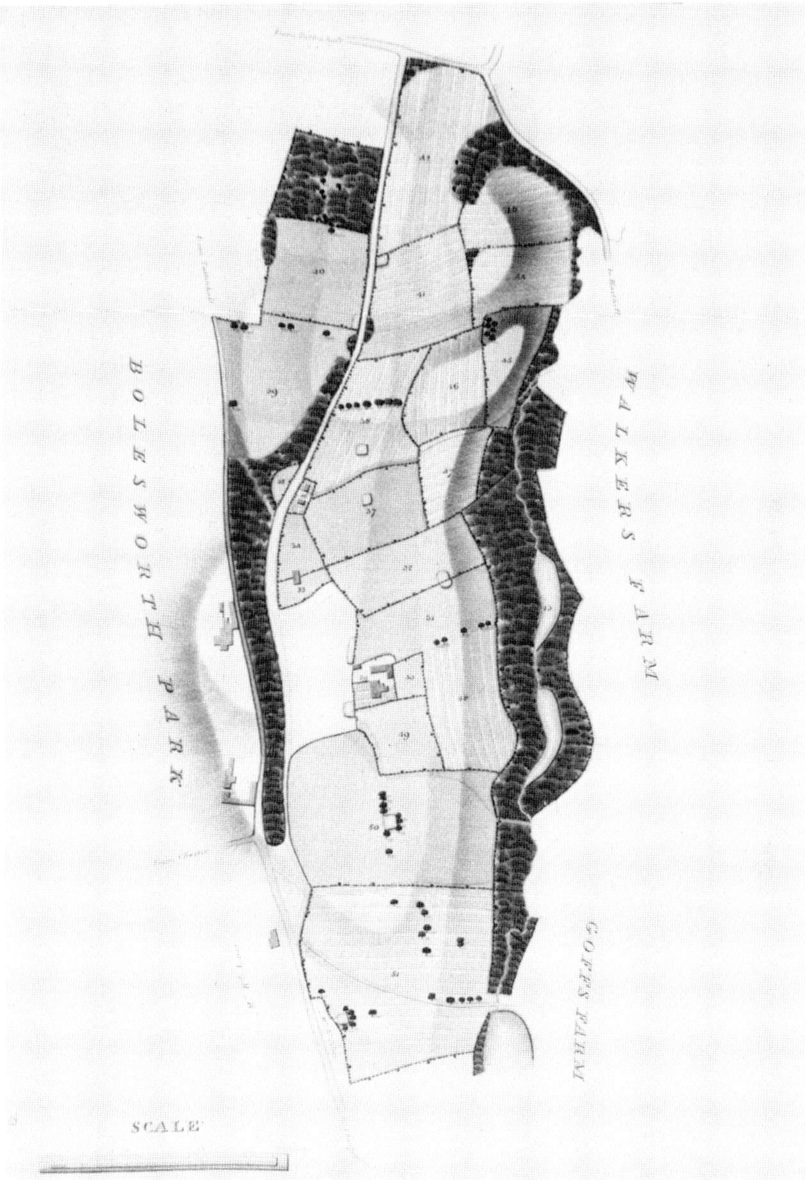

1. Map by G M Elliot, 1826, of part of the Bolesworth Estate. By kind permission of A G Barbour Esq.

The detailed map of Delamere Forest printed by order of the House of Commons in 1848, was based on a map drawn by E Fuller in 1817 which had been revised and corrected by John Palin, Surveyor, of Chester in 1848. This plan, scale 22½ chains to an inch, contains a wealth of detail including tree species planted, the woodmens' lodges, nursery, and surrounding ownerships.

All the estate plans seen are mapped on different scales, and every estate appears to have employed a different surveyor. The period 1700-1850 must have surely been boom time for agricultural surveying, and surveying generally for this was the period during which the canals and then many of the railways were planned and constructed.

Care needs to be taken interpreting acreages for the Cheshire acre was widely used in the 18th century and it is equal to 2.13 statute acres. Some maps give both. The Badeslade 1737-8 Grosvenor Estate map of Belgrave for instance, shows Belgrave Wood as 9 acres 3 roods 21 square poles statute acres and 4.2.25 Cheshire acres, and Belgrave Coppice as 4.0.0 statute acres or 1.3.22 Cheshire acres.

Pictures

The best known bird's eye views are those of Dunham Massey, where Kip's 1697 engraving of the hall, gardens, and park pictured from the south, can be compared with a series of views painted by John Harries in 1751 after the 2nd Earl of Warrington had planted and landscaped the park. Recently John Phibbs has used these to help him work out the planting patterns used so that the National Trust can carry out a phased replanting programme which conforms to the original design.

Peter Tilleman's bird's eye view of Combermere at the end of the 17th century looks across the mere to the parkland and woodland beyond, and shows rough shooting in progress. Kip's 1712-14 view of Eaton Hall shows the garden layout and surrounds.

Thomas Bardwell painted views of Adlington around 1760 which illustrate the landscape at that time, very different from today as the lake to the north of the hall is now woodland screening it off from the road.

George Stubbs painted scenes for the 1st Earl Grosvenor, including his well-known painting of the Grosvenor Hunt, 1762, showing wild boar, horses and hounds, with the River Dee, Cheshire plain, Peckforton Hills and Rawhead in the background, but he also painted pictures of the stud which show old oak trees, some of which are still standing today not far from the estate office.

Piers Egerton-Warburton painted many water colours of Arley and its surrounds in the late 19th century, charming scenes which were accurately portrayed including one showing the tulip tree on Arley Green.

These are but a few examples of the wealth of art depicting past landscapes in Cheshire.

2. George Stubbs painting, *Mare and Foals*, showing old oaks at Eaton Stud, c 1766. By kind permission of Anne, Duchess of Westminster.

3. The nearest oak is said to be one of those depicted in the Stubbs painting, the other fell some years ago.

Estate Documents And Records

These provide the main source of information on the working detail of estate woodlands from the 17th century, but they are rarely complete except for limited periods, occasionally illegible, and often distributed among a number of libraries and record offices.

The terriers or rent rolls can prove particularly useful if remarks and snippets of information are added in. For instance the Doddington terrier of 1762, entitled *Sir B Broughton-Delve's lands*, includes remarks on the condition of some woods and coppices and suggestions for their treatment [8].

Other Sources

Some descriptions of the Cheshire landscape, including Delamere and the use of wood in the salt industry, were given in John Leland's account of his early 16th century itinerary. Celia Fiennes, who rode through the country by horse and passed through Cheshire in 1698, together with other later travellers have described aspects of county life and the landscape.

There are numerous other sources of woodland history information varying from diaries and correspondence and old photographs, to the reminiscences of retired estate staff.

Changes in woodlands and hedgerows over the last twenty years can often be detected from aerial photographs. The County Council commissioned photography in 1971-3 and 1983-4. It is probable that there will be further coverage to update the situation.

Finally of course there are the trees themselves. A forester can often deduce past treatment and history from the condition and form of the trees. Age can be confirmed by counting annual rings if there are tree stumps. Drought years might be deduced from the closeness of two successive rings, while a sudden and sustained widening of the rings could be the response to thinning or the canopy opening in some way.

CHAPTER 4 - Early Woodland Management

After more than 5000 years of human interference ancient natural woodland had been reduced to but a few relics, but woodland management and plantation forestry have slowly evolved over the centuries.

Trees have been introduced from other countries which are now an important part of the woodland scene. The English elm, *Ulmus procera*, was a particularly interesting introduction for it is believed to have been brought in originally by Iron Age tribes to the south of England. It was planted around settlements and along boundaries where the sucker growth was valuable in maintaining a permanent boundary, while the tree itself produced useful fodder. This tree was a feature of parts of the Cheshire countryside until recent years when elm disease killed off almost the entire stock of semi-mature and mature trees in the county. Fortunately the truly native elm, the wych elm, *Ulmus glabra*, is more resistant to the disease, but even so many have been lost. The white poplar, *Populus alba*, and the grey poplar, *Populus canescens,* are thought to be earlier introductions, while the sweet chestnut, *Castanea sativa,* was brought in by the Romans [1].

Even before Norman times there were two traditional ways of managing woodland, either as coppice or as pasture woodland [2]. The oldest tradition was coppice in which a continual supply of wood of small size can be obtained by cutting the trees on a regular rotational basis and allowing the stools to regenerate. Hazel coppice could be cut every seven to ten years, while other species like oak, ash, alder, birch would be cut at slightly longer intervals, though in any cutting all the trees were felled at the same time.

During Medieval times a system gradually developed in which a few coppice stems were left and allowed to grow on to produce larger diameter timber, usually oak or ash depending on the site. The wood then consisted of coppice underwood to produce small sized material for poles, firewood, charcoal and other needs, and widely spaced larger stems to produce timber. This dual purpose system became known as 'coppice with standards'. Coppices were divided up into 'falls' or 'panels' so that one such area was cut each year and production was perpetuated.

The coppice regrowth had to be protected from grazing when young, so there was normally a hedge or paling to protect the boundaries of each area of young coppice. As the coppice got older stock could be allowed in for grazing woodland and ride, so in effect there was a rotational system of grazing as well as cutting [3]. Coppice underwood and overwood were legally separate items and were often owned or leased by separate people.

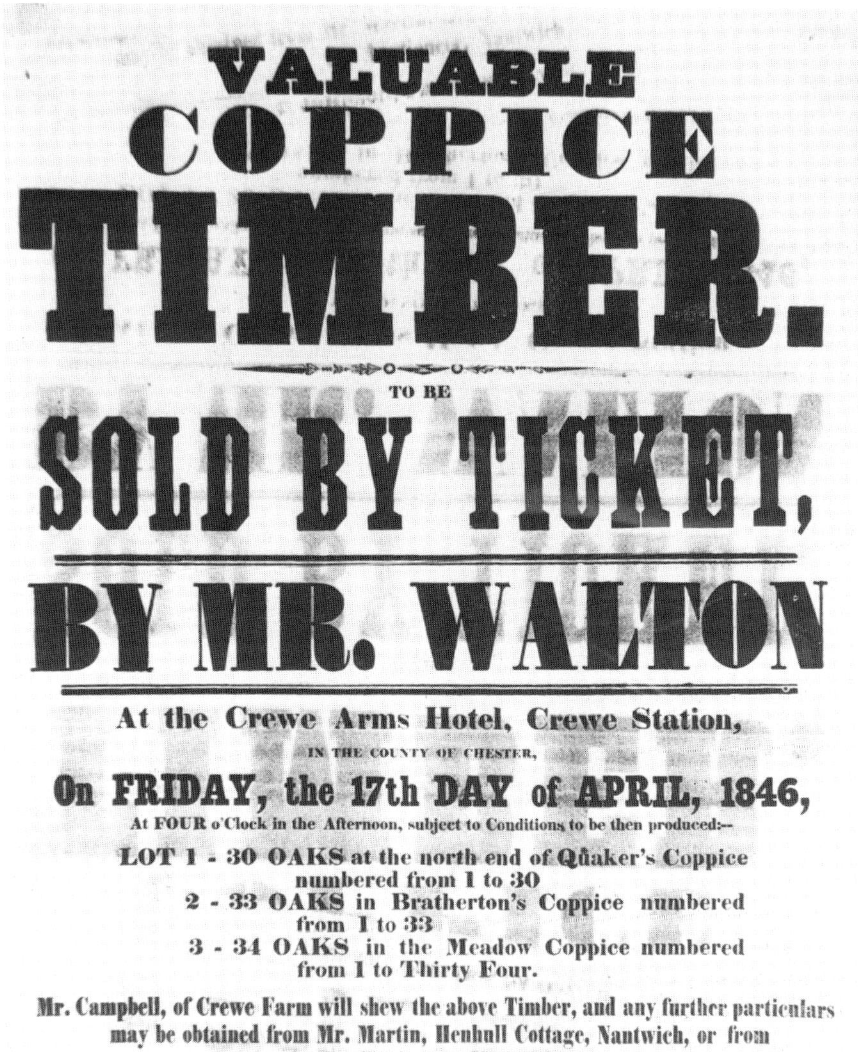
VALUABLE
COPPICE
TIMBER.

TO BE

SOLD BY TICKET,

BY MR. WALTON

At the Crewe Arms Hotel, Crewe Station,

IN THE COUNTY OF CHESTER,

On FRIDAY, the 17th DAY of APRIL, 1846,

At FOUR o'Clock in the Afternoon, subject to Conditions to be then produced:--

LOT 1 - 30 OAKS at the north end of Qûaker's Coppice numbered from 1 to 30

2 - 33 OAKS in Bratherton's Coppice numbered from 1 to 33

3 - 34 OAKS in the Meadow Coppice numbered from 1 to Thirty Four.

Mr. Campbell, of Crewe Farm will shew the above Timber, and any further particulars may be obtained from Mr. Martin, Henhull Cottage, Nantwich, or from the Auctioneer, Nantwich.

T. JOHNSON, PRINTER, NANTWICH.

4. Evidence of more coppices in the 19th century is given by this Sale of Timber Standards. Cheshire CRO DCR13/14

It was the underwood that supplied the basic necessities of life, the fuel, material for fencing, hurdles and tools, as well as rods for wattle and daub, building and roofing poles. It also met the fuel needs of early industries. The overwood, almost always oak, produced the material for the timber frames so characteristic of many old buildings in Cheshire, as well as timber for mills and bridges. Oak comprised more than 90% of building timber and the majority of trees used were in the 25-100 year age bracket of comparatively small dimensions in ordinary medieval buildings[4].

Coppice woodlands are still a feature of Shropshire, though not now managed as such, but there is not the same tradition in Cheshire where agricultural pressures have prevailed. As the demand for firewood for the salt industry fell as it was replaced by coal in the 17th century and the iron industry's requirement for charcoal lessened in the 18th century, areas of coppice declined in the county. Undoubtedly the system was widely practised before then.

The other traditional form of management was as pasture woodland, or what might be termed range management today. In this method widely spaced trees grew over pasture land and provided shelter for stock. Trees were often pollarded, that is, cut regularly at six to ten feet above ground level so that the new shoots are out of reach of deer, cattle, or other stock. They are cut on a regular basis to provide fodder, fuel, poles, and other small produce. Pollarding is an ancient practice and if carried out regularly it greatly extends the life of the tree. The trunk of a pollard was known as a bolling [5]. Bollinshurst Wood at Lyme Park was probably named after a pollard wood. In some cases shredding was practised instead of pollarding, when side branches up the trunk of the tree were regularly cut to provide a supply of fodder, fuel, and poles. A few of the very old oak in the park at Dunham Massey look as if they may have been shredded in the past.

Areas within Delamere, Macclesfield, and the Wirral Forests would have been managed as pasture woodland where both deer and commoners' stock grazed, together with imparkments within. The Cistercians were well organised land managers. At Combermere where the abbey was founded in 1133, its grange at Wincle, and Vale Royal Abbey, both pasture woodland and coppice would have been managed on a sustained and orderly basis.

In 1398, Richard II granted the manor of Lyme Handley to Piers de Legh and Margaret his wife, but reserved the oaks growing there. There was a large area of woodland for the inquisition postmortem of Peter Legh in 1542 gives 1000 acres as the quantity at Handley [6]. The oaks could have been the standards in coppice with standards woodland, bollins, or just any oak that happened to be growing in the manor. Obviously they were valuable trees as they were reserved.

In the 15th century, there was concern that timber demands were increasing and supplies were diminishing, and in 1482 an Act was passed which allowed owners of woodland lying within the bounds of a forest to enclose felled areas for a period of seven years in order to allow the young growth to get away. Further steps were taken in 1543 when Henry VIII passed an Act for the preservation of woods [7]. This Act laid down the law on coppice with standards and emphasised the importance of oak for building, shipping, furniture making, and other uses. It ordered that when coppice was felled of 24 years or less, 12 oaks known as standils or storers should be left per acre, and if there was insufficient oak to make the count elm, ash, aspen, or beech should be left to make up the number. The standils were not to be felled until they reached a size of 10 inches square within 3 feet of the ground. The Act also referred to the felling and weeding of great trees, or thinning as it is now termed.

This was an important point in the history of British forestry for it was the first step to formally regularising a system of forest management.

There were considerable areas of demesne woods by the end of the 15th century. For instance in Macclesfield Forest in the reign of Henry VII (1485-1509), when the Earl of Derby was chief forester, representatives of the families of Vernon, Hyde, Warren, Legh, Downes, Fitton, and Sutton held demesne woods [8]. The woods of Legh of Adlington began near Poynton and extended as far as Styperson Park and Hall. The demesne woods of Downes commenced on the eastern boundary of Styperson and extended from Pott to Kerridge. Warren's wood began on the

5. Recent pollarding of willows at Nantwich.

northern boundary of Adlington wood and stretched towards Norbury. After a little intervening territory the demesne wood of Vernon began and extended to Wybersley near Disley. The demesne wood of Sutton situated in Bosley was joined by that of Fitton of Gawsworth on the extreme southermost boundary of Macclesfield Forest.

It was in these and other demesne woods and imparkments throughout the county where the traditions of estate forestry developed. Medieval parks were not ornamental, they were functional enclosed areas producing meat, timber, and fuel, from areas of woodland and woodpasture [9]. William Brereton of Malpas (1490-1536) recognised the importance of his woodlands for the systematic exploitation of fuel and pannage of swine, while his concern with deer as a woodland crop was shown by his careful attention to the profits and to the upkeep of the several parks there were on his properties [10].

There is no evidence in Cheshire of any plantations of trees being established in the 15th and 16th centuries, though no doubt a number of different fruit trees and walnut, *Juglans regia*, which was said to have been introduced in pre-Roman times, were planted. Two important forest trees, the sycamore, *Acer pseudoplatanus*, and the first of the conifers to be introduced the Norway spruce, *Picea abies*, had been brought into the country by around 1500 [11]. There is no evidence that either of these trees were planted in Cheshire until the 18th century, but it is interesting to note that the Norway spruce had been a constituent of our vegetation in early interglacial times.

CHAPTER 5 - The Royal Forests

The ancient forests in Cheshire, Mara and Mondrem in the centre of the county, Macclesfield in the east, and Wirral in the peninsula, were four of the many vast tracts of land which the king designated as forest throughout the country about the time of Domesday.

Domesday itself makes no reference to forests by name, though the Earl had placed land which was waste into his forest. This was to become part of the Mara, which was the old name for Delamere.

Manwood in his *Treatise Of The Laws Of The Forest* in 1598 defined forest as

> ... a certain territory of woody grounds and fruitful pastures, privileged for wild beasts and fowls of forest, chase, and warren, to rest and abide in, for the safe protection of the king, for his princely delight and pleasure, which territory of ground, so privileged is meered and bounded with unremovable marks, meers, and boundaries, either known by matter of record, or else by prescription: and with great coverts of vert, for the succour of the said wildbeasts, to have their abode in: For the preservation and continuance of which said place, together with the vert and venison, there are certain laws and privileges, that are only proper unto a forest and not to any other place.

Forests were extensive areas of unenclosed land with recognised boundaries made up of woods, wasteland, farmland and pasture, including villages and scattered rural population. The king had exclusive rights to hunting in the forest which was protected by a series of forest laws. Those living in the forest had to abide by these as well as common law. Part of the land was owned by the king as demesne and part by the inhabitants. No doubt it was from some of these areas that many were recruited to join the huge armies of woodcutters which were assembled in Chester before proceeding to North Wales to carry out clearance operations in the campaigns of 1277, 1282-3 and 1294-5 [1].

Though a considerable part of Cheshire was taken up by the four forests, only a proportion of them were wooded. The frequency of the suffix 'ley' to place names in the forest suggests that there were many small woodland clearance settlements before the royal forests were designated. Revenue to the crown came from customary payments for privileges, assarts, or clearances, fines, the sale of timber and many other items.

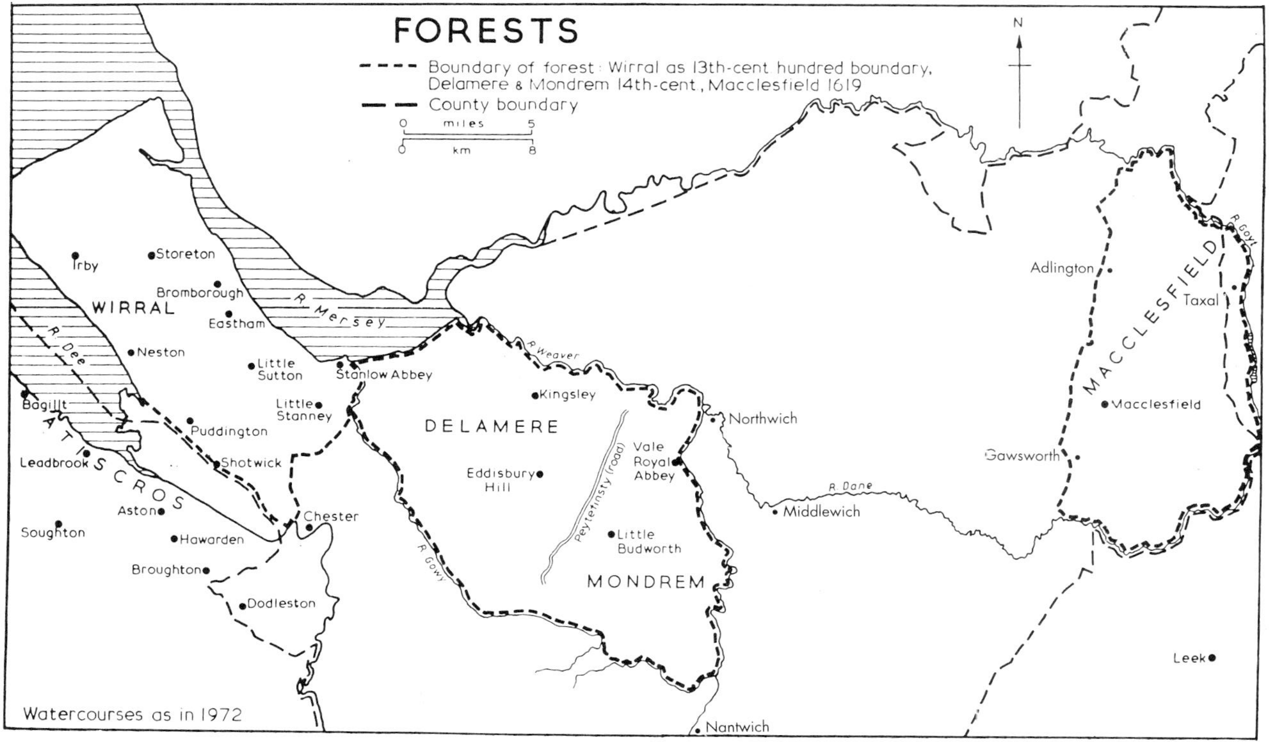

6. The Royal Forests and Early Salt Towns.
Based on the VCH Vol. II Map of the Royal Estates. By kind permission of the General Editor.

Delamere and Mondrem

These two forests lay next to each other in the centre of the county, divided by an old road called Peytefinsty which linked Tarporley with Weaverham. The forests were situated between the rivers Mersey in the north, Gowy in the west, Weaver in the east, and a tributary of the latter in the south, though the precise boundaries are not known [2]. This covers the whole of Eddisbury Hundred and most of Nantwich Hundred.

There were few recorded settlements in the upland parts in 1086, but many assarts are recorded on the forest rolls in the 13th and 14th centuries so there was continual clearance and settlement taking place and it was a constantly changing landscape.

Though only part wooded, the forest was a valuable source of oak timber for building. Oaks had gone to repair the Dee Mills in Chester, to repair Beeston Castle in 1303-4, while the Black Prince had made gifts of oak to clerks and men who had worked and fought with him. Oaks had been used also in the building of Vale Royal Abbey late in the 13th century.

The Black Prince had also been concerned about the state of the woodland and available timber in the 14th century when he strictly regulated the felling of timber from the forest, and tried to ensure that Vale Royal Abbey did not abuse its privilege of taking housebote. Housebote was the right to take timber for house building and repairs [3].

Religious houses had special privileges. Vale Royal Abbey was built at the end of the 13th century within the forest area and building timbers came from Delamere and Mondrem and stone was quarried on Eddisbury Hill. The Vale Royal manors of Darnhall, Over, Weaverham, and Conersley were disafforested and the abbey had the right to take estovers, housebote, and wood needed for glassmaking. The abbey's many and various ongoing requirements for firewood, charcoal, and timber for repairs were met by the forest [4].

St Werburgh's, Chester was also granted rights including one of hunting in the Cheshire forests granted in 1153. This was surrendered in 1285 for the right to take six bucks and six does yearly in Delamere, but the abbot's right to a tithe on all venison taken from the Cheshire forests by the king and his men was confirmed in the same year. Other rights included one to have two cartloads of deadwood for the abbey kitchen daily from the Delamere except during the close month [5].

In 1299, the Bishop of Coventry and Lichfield was licensed to impark his wood at Tarvin, and was given deer to stock the park.

There is no information about the deer population at Mondrem, but there are references to both red and fallow deer in Delamere from the 13th century. In 1252, the population was large enough for Henry III to send agents to take 100 bucks from Delamere for his use in Darnhall and Macclesfield Parks [6]. A large enclosure was made in 1337 to hold deer which included Eddisbury Camp and was about 450 acres in extent. This was the Old Pale [7]. A further area of about 340 acres, the New Pale, was enclosed three centuries later [8]. Many gifts of deer were made particularly in the 13th and 14th centuries.

It is not certain how often the earls of Chester hunted, but James I when he came and hunted in 1617, knighted John Done, the Head Forester [9]. In 1626, Sir John Done reported that 60 to 80 deer were killed annually.

However the deer population was wiped out in the Civil War. The possibility of restocking the forest was considered in 1661 but this was not done as the soil was barren and there was no shelter for the deer, since there were scarcely any trees left except for fuel [10].

In 1627, it was reported that the only timber felled was for the use of the chamberlain and judges at Chester. It was estimated that there were about 2200 oaks in Delamere at the start of the Civil War [11].

A survey in 1627 showed that the forest boundaries had contracted to exclude Mondrem. Out of a total area of 12672 acres, 8346 were unenclosed and belonged to the king. There were few changes until Delamere was disafforested in the early 19th century [12].

Macclesfield Forest

The earliest know reference to Macclesfield Forest is given in the charter issued between 1153 and 1160 by which Earl Hugh II granted Anhus to Richard Davenport by the service of forestry in fee and appointed Richard supreme forester of the Earl's forest of Leek and Macclesfield. The forest of Leek was detached from Macclesfield in the 13th century [13].

The first dated description of the forest boundary was made in 1619. The north, east and south boundaries of the forest are clearly defined by the rivers Mersey, Goyt, and Dane, but the western boundary is not clearly defined for in some cases it runs through townships and not along their boundaries or along any definite natural feature [14].

The townships lying entirely within the manor and forest are as follows:- Disley Stanley, Marple, Offerton, Taxall, Lyme Hanley, Yeardsley Whaley, Bollington, Hurdsfield, Kettleshulme, Pott Shrigley, Rainow, Sutton, Tytherington, Upton, Macclesfield Forest, Wildboarclough, Wincle and Bosley. Those lying partly wihin the forest are:- Macclesfield, Adlington, Butley, Gawsworth, Poynton, Prestbury, North Rode, Norbury and Torkington [15].

The area of the forest was approximately 95 square miles. It contained farmland, villages, woodland, hill, pasture, and wasteland, supporting a scattered but small rural population. A considerable part of it is upland moorland where few settlements were recorded in 1086. There were some extensive areas of woodland recorded in Domesday included under the Earl's manors of Macclesfield 6 leagues by 4, and Adlingon 11 leagues by 2, but no mention of Macclesfield Forest [16].

The forest had been in existence prior to Domesday when it was known as the Forest of Lyme. Hunting had always been important and the forest was constantly restocked with deer until the restoration. Before the Civil War, about 200 head were maintained for the King's use [17], but it was not known how frequently it was used, though Edward I had hunted there a long time previously in 1290 [18].

The forest was not enclosed though there were enclosures within it which included the Coombs where the deer were preserved first mentioned in 1291 [19]. Some licenses to impark were given such as that granted in 1642 to Robert Legh of Adlington for enclosing Adlington Wood, Whiteley Green, and Heys [20]. Examination of the court rolls bears out the mixed land usage of the forest area and gives some indication of the agricultural and forest practices. Curry noted that Macclesfield inhabitants were widely involved in farming activity in the forest in the 15th century [21].

Some old boundary marks of ancient origin which may have been connected with the forest at a later date are recorded by Ormerod [22]. The Bow Stone is situated at the gate to Lyme Park about two miles southwest of Disley and there are others called the Cross o' the Moor in Sutton, the Clulow Cross in Wincle and a cross on the boundary between Upton and Fallibroome about a mile from Macclesfield.

The landscape changed through assarting, imparkment, and encroachment over the years. A commission of enquiry ordered by Cardinal Wolsey in the early 16th century found that about half the forest was occupied by settlers, that farms had been established, and that sheepfolds and fields had been taken from the forest land. An example is cited at Raynowe "... by estimation in length from the Black Lowe to a place called the Brink a myle and in breadth from the forest side to Macclesfield two myles "[23].

Many of the townships in the forest had customary rights and in 1285 Bosley, Bollington, Adlingon, Poynton, Norbury, Heppales, Torkington, Rode and Gawsworth successfully defended their right to take oaks from their demesne woods without view of the foresters [24].

Gifts of oak were sometimes made such as the 23 trees given by the Black Prince in 1365 to five men whose houses had fallen down while they were with the prince in Aquitaine.

Charcoal was made in the forest for the Crown Revenue Accounts pre 1560 detail that no fines were taken from the charcoal burners in the forest of Macclesfield [25].

A considerable proportion of the forest consisted of inhospitable hill ground on the Pennines and this together with agricultural pressure for grazing, limited the area under woodland. Perhaps Manwood's great coverts of vert were comparatively small and were most likely to be found on poor agricultural ground, rough hill slopes, and steeply sided valleys. The lower ground may have been more densely covered.

The forest was attached to the Earldom of Chester until it terminated when it passed to the crown. In 1684 when the Earl of Derby acquired pastures that had been leased to him by the Earls of Chester since the 15th century, the forest came to an end except as an administrative area [26]. The sporting value of the forest had declined over the years as the main alternative landuse, agriculture, developed.

The Forest of Wirral

This covered the whole of the Wirral and is said to have come into being around 1129. One of the reasons for designation could have been to exert more control on a recalcitrant local population and to obtain revenue from extra fines and taxation. The earliest documentary evidence of the forest is a charter of Ranulph III, issued between 1194 and 1208, which released the freemen of Wirral from maintaining serjeants of the peace other than six foresters on foot, unless circumstances required otherwise [27].

At Domesday there were few references to woodland and the land was more densely populated than the other forest areas at the time. St Werburgh's Abbey had four manors in the forest, Eastham, Bromborough, Irby and Sutton, and abbots were often found assarting land, cutting down timber, and digging marlpits. The abbey's privileges included exemption from the foresters' puture, that is the goods or money that foresters were normally entitled to claim [28].

The forest was stocked with both red and fallow deer which were sometimes taken for the earl, but no reference has been found to any hunting by the earl in the forest, or to any hunting lodge [29].

The state of the woodland within the forest was causing concern as early as 1251 and many cases of felling trees were reported at the eyre, the supreme forest court, in 1347. The Black Prince imposed strict controls in 1351 to prevent destruction of the vert [30]. An indication that there was a shortage of wood is given by the concession the Prince made to the Head Forester, William Stanley, in 1358, when he was allowed to take four oaks from Greves in Puddington because he had heard that William had no wood for fuel in the forest [31].

Many complaints were made by Chester citizens to the Black Prince about the lawlessness of the forest inhabitants and those that took refuge in the forest after raiding and plundering. Eventually in 1376, just before the death of the Black Prince, Wirral was disafforested by charter of Edward III [32].

There is an old saying:-

From Blacon Point to Hilbree,
A squirrel may leap from tree to tree

This infers that the Wirral was densely wooded in the middle ages but there is little evidence to support it.

Chapter 6 - Early Wood Consuming Industries

The woodlands of Cheshire have served the needs of industry for fuel and timber over the centuries.

Salt

The Domesday Book provides the first written account of the salt industry in Cheshire with references to Middlewich, Nantwich and Northwich and the customs and laws applicable to each [1]. Unfortunately, there is no mention of wood supply though at Droitwich, which was the main inland centre for salt production, Domesday states that wood supply was the responsibility of the holding manor. It is likely, but not certain, that similar arrangements applied to the Cheshire wiches.

Wood was used as fuel to boil the brine and crystallise out the salt. It was the mandatory fuel for heating salt pans of lead which, if used with care over a wood fire, would last indefinitely. Charcoal and fossil coal were more efficient fuels but they were unsuited to lead pans for there was danger of the metal melting [2].

In the early 16th century, Leland estimated that 6000 loads of wood were used each year in salt making in Droitwich. He made no comparative statement for Cheshire when he toured the county though he did note the '... great stakkes of smaul clovyn wood' piled outside each Northwich wich-house. If it is assumed that each cartload at Droitwich contains 0.8 cubic metres of firewood, 800 hectares of well managed coppice would have been needed to supply the industry there on a sustained basis. If Cheshire production was 25% that of Droitwich, 200 hectares or 500 acres of coppice woodland could have met the demand annually, until coal started to be used in the 17th century. The change took place in Northwich and Middlewich between 1620 and 1640, but lead pans and thus fuelwood continued to be used in Nantwich until 1696. An argument put forward by a Nantwich salt owner was that more wood was needed to produce charcoal to make an iron pan, than that needed for the lead pan it would replace [3].

Though some of the fuelwood may have come from clearances and the tops of trees felled for timber, it seems certain that the bulk of the supply came from coppice woodland managed for the production of fuel. King in his *Vale Royal of England*, 1656, mentions this management:

> ... and Awstaston where he had goodly woods that have been the chief store house and nursery of that fewd they call wichwood which being of twenty years of thereabouts is most fit for that service and hath usually been

> fallen by yearly falls as they call them and sold to the town of Namptwich for the boyling of salt.

Austerson is about three miles south of Nantwich and in Domesday it is recorded as having woodland 1 league long and 1/2 wide [4].

It is probable that the woodfuel needs of the salt industry were met from woodland within five miles of the salt towns. The needs of the industry were longstanding and would have led to sustained and systematic management of blocks of coppice woodland close by.

There were many other requirements for wood in the salt towns. Brine was transported in wooden channels and pipes to the salt houses, where it was stored in wooden ships, hollowed out tree trunks, or barrels, to await transfer to the lead pans for boiling [5]. Elm was the favoured species for wooden piping and vessels for it is resistant to liquids and is long lasting. Wood was used for many of the traditional tools of the trade and the wich house construction. Two of these houses were

7. The use of timber in the salt industry; transferring salt from a canal boat to a chute for loading a Weaver Flat. Photograph by the late Fred Done.

excavated in Nantwich in 1980. Both were barn like structures, one constructed with a double wall of stakes and the other being timber framed with five massive posts down each side. Both had yards at the front of the house that provided direct access onto Wood Street and a convenient depot for storing the fuelwood. Tree ring dating of the wooden posts gave a date of 1170-1190 for the timber framed building, the other may have been earlier [6]. The complex was previously known as Great Wood Street, which may have led out to the main source of wood supply.

The wood needs of the industry plummeted when coal replaced wood as the fuel in the 17th century, though there were still the needs for toolmaking and building installations.

Growth of the salt industry in the 18th and 19th centuries created new needs for timber for larger installations, while boats and barges were needed to both take out the salt and bring in coal along the newly constructed canals and the improved Weaver. Improvements in transportation also provided the opportunity for importing timber, particularly deal, so not all the timber used was home grown.

An illustrated account of the history of saltmaking in the county can be seen at the Salt Museum, Northwich.

Glassmaking

Early glassmaking was a forest based industry for fuel was required to heat the furnaces, while potash, an essential ingredient in the process, was obtained from woodash or bracken. In Elizabethan times, the increased demand for wood for a multitude of purposes, but particularly for iron smelting and salt making, pushed up fuelwood prices and strained available supplies. In 1615, King James I, anxious to preserve the forests, decreed that glass was only to be made in coal fired furnaces.

Vale Royal Abbey had some special privileges in Delamere Forest which included the use of produce for glassmaking [7]. In the abbey ledger book in 1346-7 there is a complaint against Warren le Grosvenour for encroaching on abbey lands naming Le Huvyng and the whole wood towards the glassworks next Heytelegh [8]. A man named Henry de Glasshouse held a tenement in Kingsley in the late 13th century. Presumably he had been associated with glassmaking.

Vale Royal Abbey was involved in glassmaking from 1284-1309 and probably later, but the location of the glassmaking site is still uncertain. It could have been situated near Kingswood for a farmer digging a hole for the foundations of a water ram about 1/2 mile due east of New Pale Farm found evidence of a site which was subsequently excavated in 1935 and 1947. The location is known locally as Glaziers Hollow or Glaziers Brook.

Among the finds of glass and pottery on the site was carbonised wood of oak and birch, two of the principal species in the forest. Further work was carried out on the site in 1971 and later, but the exact position of the furnace has still not been located.

In the 1935 excavation 'Jones the Forester' found a silver penny of Edward I (1272-1307), which might give an indication of the date of occupation [9].

There is no evidence of extensive glassmaking activity in Cheshire woodlands, so the demands for fuel for furnaces would have been small. Once coal was used for firing the furnaces there was no need to site the process in or near woodland. St Helens became one of the centres for making glass owing to its proximity to suitable sand and coal. The history of the industry can be seen at the Pilkington Glass Museum, St Helens.

The Leather Trade

This was an important industry in the county for there were plentiful hides to be had, ample water supplies, and a ready supply of oak trees to provide the bark for tanning the leather. Bark from other tree species was also used, including alder, birch, and willow, and larch from the 19th century on when it was grown in Cheshire. Oak bark was favoured and commanded a higher price for it was consistently higher in tannin content.

It has been estimated that ten hundredweight of bark yields one hundredweight of tannin, which was sufficient to treat two hundredweight of fresh skins [10]. The bark was steeped in water-filled pits in which hides were soaked for several months.

The leather trade in Cheshire was particularly important in the 17th and 18th centuries in the central and northern part of the county. Shoes and gloves were made in Congleton, Nantwich, and Sandbach [11]. Chester tanyards were concentrated in Foregate Street and Bakers Lane but they were hard hit by tax on tanned hides in 1711 [12].

Bark was shipped to Ireland which enabled the Irish to tan their own leather. Between 1703-13 Cheshire tanners objected to this and demanded that the bark be withheld in order to force the Irish to send raw hides to Cheshire so that they had sufficient hides for the available bark. Evidently the balance between pasture and woodland was not in equilibrium [13]. Demands for halting exports and removing tax were unsuccessful.

Tanyards were situated throughout the county. Field names may give a clue to old sites. Barkmill Brown is shown on a 1754 map of lands at Sutton just east of a small wood unnamed then, but marked as Low's Wood in the current 1: 25000 OS Map.

An old method of treating oak bark described in 1793 was to grind it down with a heavy stone wheel turned by a horse. This was universally used but several now use cast iron cylinders between which the bark is passed, being more efficient and requiring less labour [14].

The sale of bark for tanning was an important source of revenue for the woodland owner, often fetching as much as the timber it was stripped from. Prices rose to around £12 per ton for oak bark during the Napoleonic wars. Bark is easiest to peel in the spring when the sap is rising so trees were sometimes peeled standing and felled the following autumn, for winter felled timber was more valuable. However this was not always possible. Because of the close relationship of bark and timber, some tanners were also timber merchants such as Mr William Wright of Runcorn, Tanner, who bought a parcel of timber at Malpas Hall Farm in March 1819 from the Marquess of Cholmondeley [15].

Edlin describes the tool for removing bark, the barking iron. It has a spade-like handle and a narrow chisel pointed blade. Hatchets were used to cut the bark across the trunk top and bottom, vertical slits were made with the barking iron joining the cuts, and the bark was then levered off in long strips [16]. Barking spades are still in use in the forest for peeling logs, but the job is normally carried out with a mechanical peeler.

In the 20th century extracts from tropical timbers and chemical substitutes were introduced into the industry, as in most cases they were cheaper and often more efficient. These gradually replaced the use of bark collected from our own forests. Now only one or two small specialist markets for bark and tanning remain, but there are none in Cheshire.

Copper Mining

Mining activity on a small scale was carried out on Alderley Edge over 3000 years ago, for working tools dating back to that time were found in old workings. The mines could have been in use during the Roman occupation but this is not yet proven [17]. Production has been intermittent over the years finally coming to an end in the 1914 18 war. There was also a small mine at nearby Mottram St Andrew.

Copper ores were treated on site or smelted in open hearth furnaces using charcoal, until coal fired furnaces started to come into use early in the 18th century. The wood requirements for this mining were almost entirely for fuel or charcoal making, for little timber was used down the mines where vertical pillars of rock were left for support. Areas of coppice would have been needed to meet this demand but Alderley Edge was described as not appearing to have a single tree growing on it prior to 1744 [18].

However in the Gallantry Bank mine at Bickerton, the other area where copper was mined in the county, timber was used underground. This mine was worked from about 1690 for around 200 years. In an early agreement that Sir Philip Egerton of Oulton had with two miners they were required to dig and timber the excavations with timber he provided. In a set of working rules laid down in 1697

> the steward must provide the miners always with a good quantity of several sorts of wood or timber for it happened sometimes that there needs in haste to prevent great dammage [19].

In 1690 the ore was treated on-site using charcoal furnaces [20].

It is not possible to quantify the total wood requirements for either the Alderley Edge and Mottram St Andrew mines or the Bickerton mine, but they are unlikely to have been large for production was never on a big scale.

The Iron Industry

Early iron making was concentrated in the Weald and the Forest of Dean where there were ample supplies of wood for charcoal making, the charcoal being used for smelting the ores. In the 17th century pressures on the industry in the Weald forced some ironmasters to move northwards and as early as 1619 a forge was built at Tib Green, Doddingon on the Checkley Brook. The earliest known Cheshire ironmaster John Turner opened a forge at Lea on the Checkley Brook, Warmingham on the River Wheelock, and in the Vale Royal. The latter forge was taken over by Abraham Darby but stopped production around 1733 [21].

By the mid 18th century, coke furnaces came into use as they were more economical than charcoal. They were larger and remained longer in the blast, and by the end of the century the charcoal using works were sold off.

During the Commonwealth when most of the forges came into being it is thought that some landowners sold woods to the ironmasters to raise money, but no definite evidence of this has been found.

The industry in Cheshire was never a large one so the requirement for wood to make charcoal for the forges was comparatively small when compared to other areas of the country. One statute cord of wood would produce from 4 to 5 cwts of charcoal which was sufficient to make around 0.25 tons of cast iron or 0.18 tons of bar iron [22]. Bar iron production in the early 1730s was said to be about 460 tons. Five hundred acres of coppice could produce the 2500 statute cords required annually to make sufficient charcoal to sustain bar iron production on this level. In fact production dropped to 290 tons and then rose to 600 tons by 1750 when coal fired furnaces were introduced [23].

For a short period in the 17th century there could have been competition locally in the Nantwich area between the fuelwood requirements of the salt industry and the charcoal needs of the ironmasters until coal and coke took over. Charcoal was more economical to transport than fuelwood and could come from woods a considerable distance away from the forges. However Checkley Wood, which appears from a 1792 description to have been a coppice with standards in previous years, was surely used for charcoal production with tops of timber trees and underwood being used for that purpose.

Coal Mining

In Tudor Cheshire, both adit and pit methods of coal mining were in use in the Cat and Fiddle area and the Goyt Valley mines [24]. Undoubtedly some timber was used underground. Cheshire's mining belt stretched from Macclesfield where there were largely surface workings on the common, through Pott Shrigley to Poynton where quality was much improved. Coal was also to be found at Neston on and under the Dee estuary, an extension of the Flintshire coalfield.

Early records from Poynton include a lease in 1589 for a coal pit at Worth occupied by George Finche, and in 1612 Roger Downes of Shrigley received rental for a new coalpit and coalmines in Worth [25].

At Waterloo Pit, Poynton timber stock listed in an 1826 lease included 29 oak logs, 168 scotch fir logs, 5 larch logs, and 160 alder logs, while there were oak scantlings, tub scantlings, boards and planks at many pits and 1159 pieces of postwood [26]. Much of this timber would have come from local estates and the stocklist illustrates the variety of timbers used in mining.

Since those days the mining industry in Wales and English counties close to Cheshire have provided a ready market for softwood and lower grade hardwood timber, but in the last decade with the move to more open cast mining, changing techniques, and a reduction in demand for coal, timber requirements of the mining industry are much reduced.

Shipbuilding

The demand for shipbuilding timber increased rapidly at the beginning of the 18th century. By 1700, several shipyards had become established in the vicinity of the pool, there was considerable trading activity centring on Liverpool and the Mersey was navigable as far as Warrington.

John Okill obtained the first order in Liverpool for a ship for the Royal Navy in 1739, the 44 gun *HMS Hastings*, the first ship of many orders that went to the dockyards there.

In 1720, a scheme had been enacted to make the River Weaver navigable from Frodsham Bridge to Winsford Bridge, a distance of nearly 20 miles. Vessels of 160 tonnes could then go as far as Northwich Bridge, and 100 tonnes as far as Winsford. This, combined with the construction of canals later in the century, opened up trade and industry in the county, and created a large demand for small craft. Four hundred vessels were employed navigating the Weaver solely to convey salt, and these and many other vessels had to be built and maintained.

Not all the craft were built locally, but many were, mainly by small firms. There were 36 ships of the fleet built in Liverpool in the 18th century, mostly 44 gun frigates or sloops, together with Eastindiamen and much other commercial shipping, so the requirements for timber were high [27].

John Okill (1687-1773), built 8 men-of-war in Liverpool between 1740 and 1758, and he obviously had difficulties with timber supplies [28]. Men of War were estimated to use $1^1/_2$ loads of timber equivalent to 75 cubic feet for every ton of ship,

8. Timber for building - a 15th century cruck barn at Arley Hall.

and commercial ships were estimated to use 1.2 loads or 60 cubic feet per ton of shipping. Roger Fisher, a Liverpool shipwright and timber merchant, published a book in 1763 *Heart of Oak, the British Bulwark* as he was so concerned at the shortage of suitable shipbuilding timber. In his book, he quotes John Okill who said that timber supplies from Lancashire, Cheshire, and North Wales had decreased by three quarters in the last fifty years, while William Yoxall of Nantwich estimated the figure as a half.

The principal timber used in shipbuilding was oak, but elm had its uses for it remains sound as long as it is allowed to absorb water. For this reason it was always used for the bottom of narrow boats. When composite construction came in during the 19th century, iron sides were introduced with an oak or pine keel, and elm bottom. Regional timber supplies were augmented by imports of oak and deal, and later in the 19th century with teak and tropical hardwoods. Larch also came into use in the second half of the 19th century.

When construction was entirely from timber, shipbuilding on river and canal sites was often carried out by small businesses, for only a small area of flat ground on the bank was required. There was need for a sawpit to cut up the round timber and a steaming box to bend timber components into shape, a bench and a storeshed, together with sufficient room on level ground to take the boat and a slipway.

Flats were built of oak at Northwich, Winsford, and Sankey Bridge near Warrington in the 18th and 19th centuries. A fleet of locally built wooden flats was operated by Brunner Mond & Co from Northwich in 1873 to carry salt.

Canal construction also involved the use of timber for locks and sometimes banks, with oak and elm the timbers in demand. Maintenance was also required as there was wear and tear as occurred on the Weaver Navigation at Northwich in 1759. It was ordered that 200 oak trees should be bought and 500,000 bricks be made for the construction of a new lock from Messrs Garroll & Pownall from Saltersford if so many should be thought fit for this [29].

At this time Garroll & Pownall were working a parcel of Arley Estate timber at Sutton, which was said to include 1073 oaks fit for building ships, flats, or boats when it was advertised in Adams Weekly in February 1758 [30].

Garroll & Pownall also built the 28 gun *HMS Liverpool*, launched in 1758, while Richard Golightly and J & R Fisher had built frigates and sloops for the navy. It was in the period 1758-1763 that Garroll & Pownall, and Fisher, Golightly, and Grayson were buying parcels of timber from the Arley Estate [31].

Some larger boatbuilding firms developed towards the end of the 19th century at the inland ports. One was Yarwoods of Northwich 1896-1956, which built craft for use locally and for export. For instance between 1906 and 1914 they built 18 steel-framed flats with wooden planking for the Rochdale Canal. Possibly their most well-known boat was the *La Goleta*, first home in the Fastnet Race in 1927, which had an overall length of 54 feet. The frames were made of English oak in one piece and of grown form, the keel oak, and the planking pitch pine. The sawpit of an early boatbuilder had developed into an extensive sawmill in their yard where timber was cut from logs in the round and fashioned to the finished article [32].

Seagoing commercial ships were built in Chester where one of the main sites was the Roodeye Yard situated by the railway and gas works next to the Dee. The last order at this yard was taken in 1854. Ships built rarely exceeded 600 tons but a Westindiaman the Clarendon, 800 tons, was launched in 1813. Thomas Powel and Cox were two of the past builders here, where there was a steady demand for shipbuilding timber, but requirements were far smaller than those at Liverpool.

After the Restoration, the price of a load of ship timber, which was defined as 50 cubic feet, rose from £2 to £2 15s 6d. By 1809, it was £7 5s 0d and 1815 £7 7s 0d, indicating the effect of timber shortage on price. After the Napoleonic wars it fell back to £6 per load by 1833 and remained constant until 1841.

Although iron ships were built early in the 19th century, it was some time before they came into general use. Naval experience in encounters during the American Civil War in 1862, which demonstrated the superiority of ironclads over wooden vessels, forced the change for otherwise our seapower was at an end. This was a turning point in the history of the crown forests which until then were being managed to produce oak for shipbuilding [33]. It was not so damaging to the landed estates in Cheshire who had largely been planting mixed plantations and softwoods from the mid 18th century onwards.

Though methods of construction have changed there is still a small demand today for high quality timber suitable for boatbuilding, particularly boatskin larch logs which are clean large diameter timber lengths with a swept butt.

Other Wood Requirements

There were undoubtedly other industrial needs but by far the largest requirement was wood for domestic use, particularly fuel which was a vital need in everyday life and timber for building. Alternative fuel in the form of peat from moss rooms was available in some areas when the mosses were exploited from the 17th century on, and coal was available in East Cheshire though often of poor quality. This helped to alleviate shortages as the population increased and some areas of woodland and heath were converted to agriculture.

Chapter 7 - The Development of the Nursery Trade

There is no evidence of the existence of forest or ornamental nurseries in Cheshire in the 17th century when tree planting started to become fashionable on the large estates. The beechwood planted by the mere at Alderley Hall around 1650 was said to originate from beechmast procured from Sir James Pytts of Kyre, Worcestershire [1], so presumably plants were raised in the garden at Alderley but there is no record confirming this.

It is probable that early garden designers such as George London, who drew up plans for a formal garden at Cholmondeley in 1691 [2] and laid it out near the site of the old hall, obtained plants from outside the county. He was a partner in a well-known London nursery business, Brompton Park, and it is very likely that the stock came from there.

Almost all the early nurseries were situated in the London area, though John Rea (1605-1681) ran a small nursery at Kinlet, Shropshire, and towards the end of the century John Telford bought a small and ancient nursery in York on the site of the Dominican friary, and developed a forest nursery. About the same time John Perfect had expanded a small nursery business in Pontefract, Yorkshire and was growing many forest trees [3]. These two Yorkshire nurseries secured a large part of the trade in the region and must have supplied trees to Cheshire estates in the 18th century. Certainly Arley Estate obtained 1000 grafted English elm 2½ feet high from John and William Perfect in 1756 for £7 10s 0d plus 3 bags matts and package 2s 0d and transport to Manchester 8s 4d, total £8 0s 4d [4].

Delivery of the plants, often a slow and complicated process, was well described in a letter Willoughby Ashton sent from London on November 9th 1700 to his father Sir Willoughby Ashton Bart, of Aston Hall, Cheshire [5]. This concerned the arrangements for dispatching 150 7 - 8 foot lime trees of 2 inch stem diameter from a nursery in London to Cheshire. The roots were covered in straw and bound in a mat, with a further mat around the stems in each bundle of 7 or 8 trees, A cart took them from nursery to riverside, where they were loaded onto a barge for onward transmission to the ship *Providence* which could take them to Liverpool or Nessen within 3 miles of Frodsham Bridge for collection by the estate. Transport added 50% to the cost of the plants which were just over 11d each. The letter also included advice on planting. Broken roots should be pruned with a sloping downward cut, while shag or hairlike fibres which are of the greatest use to a newly planted tree must only have their ends snipped of. If the trees are long at sea so that their roots are very dry or if it is a dry season, let the roots lie 4 or 5 hours in water before planting. Trees must not be planted deep, 6 or 7 inches above the root is enough, and fern or litter should be laid about the roots to keep off frost. If it is a dry spring one watering then is better than ten times in the summer, and finally next winter the earth should be opened up just at the top and some dung laid in.

In 1722, Mr Robert Beck, who was apparently a nurseryman in Chester, supplied 120 Scotch fir plants at 1/6 per dozen and 2 ounces of seed at 1/6 per ounce to the Chirk Castle Estate [6], so presumably the estate raised some of their own plants. Arley Estate raised poplar at a nursery at the Gore in 1755 and at a nursery at Aston Park in 1756, while at Sutton in 1764 estate workers were making fences at a poplar nursery and an ash nursery, and planting trees and guttering in Stockham Nursery [7]. John Ruffold the Arley gardener from 1759-1763, who was paid £20 per annum and lived and ate in the Hall, had trained under the Perfects of Pontefract. He would have been well versed at raising forest trees and possibly he introduced improved techniques to the estate. It is probable that it was estate practice to raise hardwoods in nurseries sited in part of the area to be planted. Plants would be moved out into the plantation and sufficient would be left behind to grow on. Oak was more often established in plantations in the 18th century by direct sowing of acorns, but early in the 19th century it was more usual to plant young oak raised in nurseries. The Dunham Massey records [8] show that considerable quantities of acorns were collected in the period 1774-1788 but there is no information of what use they were put to. In 1762, it was recommended that the Rough in Doddington should be taken in hand and sown with acorns and planted with such woods as would be agreeable to the several soils [9]. In 1757 the Royal Society for the Arts (RSA) offered awards to encourage planting and one of the specifications was for sowing acorns four bushels to the acre [10].

Landscape designers like Capability Brown (1715-1783), Humphrey Repton (1752-1818) and William Emes (1730-1783), all of whom played a considerable part in the landscaping of Cheshire estates, had connections with the nursery trade outside the county and would rarely have used locally grown stock. By 1760, a tree nursery business was established in Knutsford for Arley Estate obtained 40 large Scots fir at £3 per hundred from John Nickson who also supplied 1 Arbor vitae and 1 Tacamaha poplar for one shilling each [11].

Some years later Nickson took on a partner John Carr, to become J Nickson & Carr, Nurserymen, Knutsford. An apprentice by name William Caldwell was employed in 1780, and he became junior partner when Nickson retired in 1796. J Nickson & Carr became Carr & Caldwell [12]. Caldwell's nursery could still be found in Knutsford in 1991.

George Roberts of Chester was running the Nun garden in 1789, and by the time of his death in 1799 he had built up a sound business, leasing land at Handbridge and

Flookersbrook. The nursery passed to his wife Sarah and her son John Gorton on his death. Though they traded in forest trees it is not certain how much was raised on their own ground, for there is a record of stock being purchased from Nickson & Carr in 1796 [13].

No large nursery emerged in the Chester area until Francis Dickson established his business in 1820 in the Newton area [14]. By that time Caldwells were well established at Knutsford but the market for forest plants and trees was increasing. Dicksons developed rapidly and acquired a good reputation both inside and outside the county, producing a wide range of stock.

Some very large orders for plants in Cheshire had been supplied by nurserymen from outside the county. In 1795, a Scottish nursery near Hawick supplied 487,040 trees for planting undertaken by Sir Nicholas Ashton close to Sandiway, and in 1797, 947,650 trees were planted at Taxall [15], plant source unstated but not Caldwells.

At the first international forestry exhibition, held in Edinburgh in 1884, Chester based Dicksons obtained a gold medal for their collection of trees and shrubs. Their show advertisement read:

James Dickson & Sons
The Newton Nurseries and 108 Eastgate Street
Contract Planting To Any Extent
Their Nursery Stock Covering Upwards Of 250 Acres Of Bleak Exposed Land Offering Every Advantage To Intending Planters The Trees Being Thoroughly Hardy And Well Grown And the Quantity And Variety Unlimited.

Besides being a notable figure in public life in Chester (he was Mayor in 1885-6), George Dickson contributed to the early development of the English Aboricultural Society, forerunner of the Royal Forestry Society. He was a member of their Council in 1893 and helped to plan the Society's 15th annual meeting which was to be held in Chester in 1896. The Society had originated in the extreme north of England and even in 1896 most members were based there. Two carriages were reserved on a train from Newcastle and almost a hundred members came to the meeting in August that year. The Grosvenor Hotel was unable to meet the demand on it but the obliging manager was not caught napping and made arrangements to provide disconsolate members with suitable accommodation in the best hotels of the town, including the Queen Hotel, a palatial and well-managed establishment close to the station, the Albion Hotel in the same locality and others [16]. One of the attractions of the meeting was a visit to Dicksons nurseries described in the Journal of the English arboricultural association as follows:-

Roughly speaking, these nurseries extend to 450 acres. Forest trees are to be found there in millions, and there are very large stocks of ornamental and fruit trees, besides plants innumerable, roses and so on. Experts did not hesitate to express a very high opinion of the admirable order in which the nurseries were kept, the healthy and vigorous appearance of the stock, and the unequalled extent and variety. To attempt a bare enumeration even of what was specially noteworthy is impracticable. There were about 400 employees in the nurseries at this time, and sometimes, we were informed the numbers reach as many as 550. It is a colossal business, admirably managed.

Returning to the city the party were entertained at a luncheon in the Corn Exchange by the Messrs Dickson. Alderman G A Dickson occupied the chair.

9. In 1866, stock for planting Grosvenor Park, then known as New Park, came from Dicksons Nurseries in Chester. Eaton Estate Papers 59/15/1.

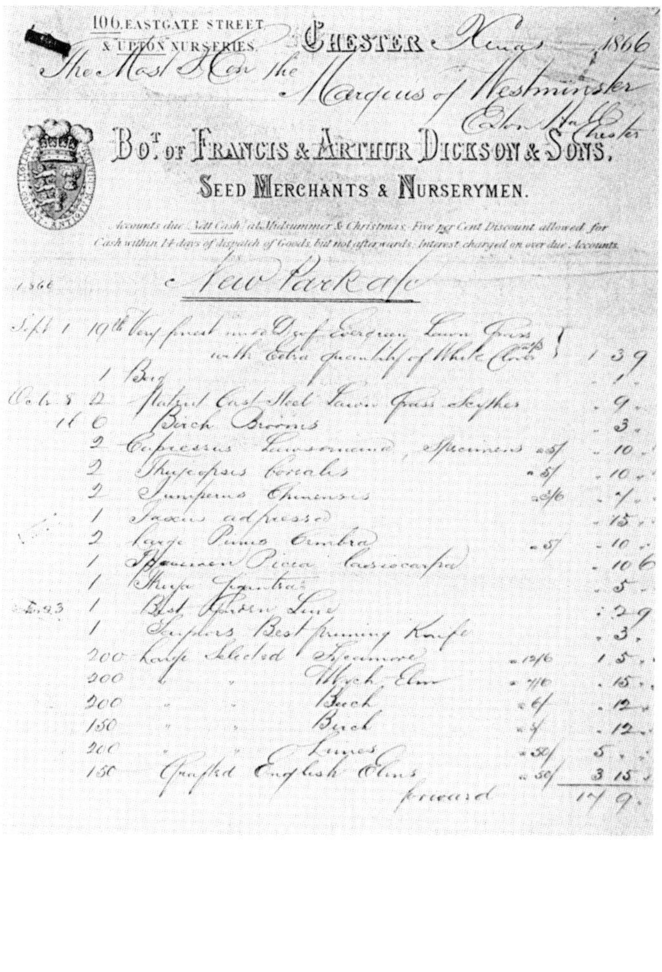

106, EASTGATE STREET & UPTON NURSERIES. CHESTER Nov 1866

The Most Hon the Marquess of Westminster Eaton Hall Chester

Bot. of Francis & Arthur Dickson & Sons,

Seed Merchants & Nurserymen.

Accounts due Nett Cash at Midsummer & Christmas. Five per Cent Discount allowed for Cash within 14 days of dispatch of Goods but not afterwards. Interest charged on over due Accounts.

New Park a/c

1866				
Sept 1	19lb	Very finest mixed Dwarf Evergreen Lawn Grass with Extra quantity of White Clover		1 3 9
	1	Bag		1 .
Oct 8	12	Patent Cast Steel Lawn Grass Scythes		9 .
16	6	Birch Brooms		3 .
	2	Cupressus Lawsoniana, Specimens	@5/	10 .
	2	Thujopsis borealis	@5/	10 .
	2	Juniperus Chinensis	@3/6	7 .
	1	Taxus adpressa		15 .
	2	large Pinus Cembra	@5/	10 .
	1	Specimen Picea cassiocarpa		10 6
	1	Thuja gigantea		5 .
Dec 3	1	Best Garden Line		2 9
	1	Saynors Best pruning Knife		3 .
	200	Large Selected Sycamore	@12/6	1 5 .
	200	" " Wych Elm	@7/6	15 .
	200	" " Beech	@6/	12 .
	150	" " Birch	@4/	12 .
	200	" " Limes	@50/	5 . .
	150	Grafted English Elms	@50/	3 15 .
		forward		17 9 .

Even if the description was over enthusiastic, Dickson's Nursery was very extensive, employed a large staff, and produced a wide range of stock, including forest trees. It ceased trading as a nursery around 1930. The land is now mainly under housing with Dicksons Drive, Newton marking the site of one of the nursery blocks.

A regional nursery of importance during the first half of the 19th century was Cunningham's of Liverpool who besides providing plants locally exported large quantities of stock to the Americas and imported American plant material [17].

It is uncertain where all the stock required for the planting of Delamere Forest was obtained. Three thousand six hundred and forty seven acres were planted between 1813 and 1823 with oak being both sown and planted, and the Scots pine interplanted from 1820 on [18]. In 1819, four acres of nursery were recorded in Castle Hill and 10 acres in Linmere, while the 1848 revision of Fuller's map shows a nursery only at Castle Hill. James Brown does not describe any Nursery or make recommendations for plant supply in his 1852 report on Delamere Forest, though he includes a sum of £150 for the purchase of 300,000 two year old Scots Pine plants in his estimates for the year 1852 - 53.

Dunham Massey planting records for 1807 mention both nurseries and direct sowing. At Bothams Wood Hattersley, 8300 trees were planted together with 11 pecks of acorns and 8 pecks of ash keys; 3½ measures of acorns were set in the nursery at Styall Green and 4 measures of acorns set in the Horse Pasture Farm nursery [19].

James Beech of Shaw near Cheadle, Staffs, who also owned Beristow Hall and Pott Hall in Pott Shrigley, described the establishment of a nursery in a letter to the Royal Society for the Arts dated 28th October 1800. The nursery was sited on land which had been common and was well fallowed. He sowed half an acre of ground with acorns in the spring of 1799 at the rate of 150 acorns per square yard. He described the quantity as 12 or 13 strikes. They were planted out as they came into size. The same spring he had sowed as many ash keys as produced 50,000 plants which had been thinned out and distributed into plantations in a similar manner. Also 15 strikes of Mountain Ash berries had produced 400,000 plants. The beds for Ash and Mountain Ash had been dug and made perfectly clean [20].

There appeared to be no great difficulty in establishing a nursery and Mr Beech could have encouraged others to do the same. The term 'strike' is normally taken to mean take root. In this case it may have meant seedbed or sowings. Estates were becoming more active. A nursery was established in Poynton Coppice in 1824 to supply plants for repopulating the estate woods, and an estate survey in 1849 records 144 acres as planted with timber including Elm Beds Wood and Poynton Coppice [21].

Capesthorne Estate records show that Monks Heath Nursery was being fenced with post and rail and wire in 1861 and that it was active certainly until 1901 [22].

In the 18th and 19th centuries, commercial nurserymen travelled the country regularly, visiting estates and clients annually when they would both take orders and collect payments. On horseback or in pony and trap this was not always easy and there were risks attached. According to Sarah Winifred Caldwell's 1964 recollections of known and hearsay of the Caldwell family and history, one of the family had been held up by highwaymen when making his annual tour. Fortunately he came to no harm[23].

Many of Caldwell's old nursery records are held in the Cheshire Records Office and they provide a fascinating insight into the sorts of trees being planted on estates in Cheshire at the end of the 18th century and during the 19th century, and the cost of plants.

Both Dicksons of Chester and Caldwells provided plants and planting services if they were required. Besides their Knutsford nurseries Caldwells had an interest in a nursery in Knowsley for the period 1789-1800, and there are some records for both nurseries. However it is the Knutsford nurseries that supplied many of the Cheshire estates and typical book records [24] are as follows:-

1792 To William Egerton Esq for forest tree planting at Higmere

March 24	250 English Poplar	8ft	£4 3s 4d
	250 Elm	8ft	£4 3s 4d
	100 Scotch Fir	2ft	10s 0d
March 30	500 Larch	3ft	£5 0s 0d
	300 Scotch Fir	2ft	£1 10s 0d
	150 Hornbeam	3ft	15s 0d
April 2	100 Scotch Fir	2ft	10s 0d
April 13	20 Scotch Fir	2ft	2s 0d
			£16 13s 8d

or 1796 Rt Hon Earl of Harrington planted at Gawsworth

April 2	1500 Larch	1ft	£3 15s 0d
	1300 Larch	2ft	£6 10s 0d
	1 Large matt		1s 6d

or 1797 To John Trafford Esq Planted upon Alderley Edge

January 23	1000 Beech	2ft	£3 0s 0d
	200 Black Poplar	4ft	£2 0s 0d

200 English Elm grafted	3ft	£1 10s 0d
1000 Spruce Fir	2ft	£8 0s 0d
1000 Weymouth Pine	1-2ft	£10 0s 0d
400 Larch	3-4ft	£3 0s 0d

Seed was sometimes supplied as for example the 2 bushels of acorns provided in January 1792 to John Bower Jodrell at Henbury for 4/- per bushel, who presumably raised oak in the estate garden, though sometimes it was the practice to dibble acorns straight into the plantation. Alternatively the acorns could have been purchased for feeding swine, but this is far less likely.

However it was the first half of the 19th century when some very large orders for forest plants were received such as that supplied to Wilbraham Egerton Esq for the park at Tatton as follows:-

March 2 1830	100,000 Larch 2 year old at 2/-	£10 0s 0d
	6,000 Spruce 2 year old at 5/-	£1 10s 0d
	2,000 Balsam Guilead 2 year old at 7/6	15s 0d
	1,000 Silver Fir at 7/6	7s 6d
	3,000 Scotch Fir 2 year old at 2/6	7s 6d
a total of 112,000 forest trees costing		£13 0s 0d

The large number of repeat orders from Cheshire estates for a wide range of forest, fruit, and ornamental trees indicates that good service and quality had been maintained over the years.

Another nursery of importance in Cheshire was William Clibrans of Altrincham and Hale who operated from towards the end of the 19th century until 1968. John R Brown of Oldfield Nurseries, Altrincham reading a paper at the York meeting of the English Arboricultural Association in June 1899 on the subject of Japanese larch, said that one year he had splendid seedlings grown at Messrs Clibran. The following year the Association visited the Clibrans Nurseries and at that time there were over 75 acres of forest trees [25]. It was noted then that true native Scotch fir twice transplanted was growing in the nursery, the seed source being the Queen's Ballochbuie forests, and in addition to the English and Japanese Larch, over 100,000 Siberian larch and American larch were being grown experimentally.

Forest tree production was part of a large and successful horticultural business which had Royal Warrants going back to King Edward VII. The most recent was granted in 1955 and cancelled in 1964 when William Robert Clibran died [26].

In 1893, when Spencer Gore of Smith and Gore the agents responsible for the management of Delamere Forest at the time, put forward a replanting programme for part of the forest, quotations for plant supply were obtained from Fell of Hexham, Little and Ballantyne of Carlisle, and Dicksons of Chester. Larch, Scots pine, Corsican pine, and birch were required. The 9000 Corsican pine transplants were provided by Dicksons for 16s per 1000 [27].

In 1902, it was proposed to put seedbeds in the Delamere nursery and the following year one kilogramme each of Scots pine and Corsican pine seed was obtained from Conrad Appel, seed merchant of Darmstadt, Germany for 13s 3d including postage. A further seed order to the same merchant in 1906 included Weymouth pine [28]. Stock was still being bought in for in 1905 Clibrans supplied Scots pine and Dicksons supplied Corsican pine [29]. When E P Popert reported on Delamere forest in 1908 there were two nurseries in the forest, and he proposed that both should be retained, while to ensure sturdy and well rooted plants both should be manured from time to time [30].

The Forestry Commission took charge of Delamere Forest in 1923 and from 1924 on almost all plants used for replanting came from their nurseries in Delamere. In 1951, 34 acres were under nursery, today the area of Abbotts Moss, Lob Slack,

10. Cheshire Nurseries foreman Stuart Haggis showing six month old containerised oak seedlings.

and the Old Pale nurseries exceeds 200 acres for the nurseries supply all the Commission's requirements for broadleaved trees and the coniferous needs of the Forest Enterprise south of a line from Merseyside to the Humber which includes all Wales. These amount to an annual requirement of approximately 115 million trees. Included in this total are 2.5 million super Sitka, an improved strain of Sitka spruce vegetatively reproduced. Sitka spruce is the conifer which produces the softwood timber most demanded by industry. Also in the total are approximately 1.2 million broadleaved trees.

The Forestry Commission nursery does not normally sell any trees to the public unless there is surplus stock. However there are a number of nurseries in the county which produce containerised and cell grown stock, whips, standards and advanced nursery stock, including one which grows large trees up to ten metres in height.

There have been a number of recent developments in the nursery trade which have benefitted the forester. One of the most important has been the introduction of the cell grown plant, for the root system is undisturbed at planting and moisture is conserved in the plug of soil in which the young seedling is growing. This has enabled the planting season to be brought forward to September and extended into May. Species like the silver birch and Corsican pine are notoriously difficult to establish as open rooted transplants unless climatic conditions are particularly favourable and the use of cell grown and container stock has transformed the situation. Open rooted stock continues to be widely used and here also there have been corresponding advances including improved undercutting techniques to strengthen the root system, the introduction of cold storage facilities, and more careful handling and packaging.

Many of the large estates have operated small forest nurseries of their own for periods this century, but economics have become important, and now none remain.

Good nursery stock is one of the cornerstones of a successful plantation. Healthy stock with a well-balanced root system should be selected, originating from a favourable provenance or seed source. It is always advisable to seek professional advice on species selection, provenance, and type and size of stock to use for planting so that it meets the particular conditions and objectives of the scheme.

Chapter 8 - Forestry on the Cheshire Estates

Most estate woodland was organised on a coppice or coppice with standards system in the 17th century, which together with areas of woodland pasture met their essential requirements for timber and fuel. There was increasing national concern at the time of the restoration that the country's timber resources were depleted and in 1662, John Evelyn read his *Sylva: or, a Discourse of Forest Trees, and the Propogation of Timber in His Majestie's Dominions* to the Royal Society.

This was the first comprehensive book on forestry which described in detail how trees should be raised and grown to produce timber, and it signalled the start of a new era in which it was becoming fashionable to plant trees.

One of the first plantations in Cheshire was made by Sir Thomas Stanley at Alderley who planted beech at the Mere around 1650. It was also the first introduction of beech to the county, the mast coming from Kyre, Worcestershire. It is not certain if it was sown directly into the plantation ground, or whether plants were first raised in a nursery and then planted out [1]. Beech was also planted in the late 17th century [2].

Much of the early planting was carried out to provide impressive and attractive surrounds to halls and formal gardens. A lime avenue which led to the formal garden was planted in 1688 at Adlington. Lime was also planted at Aston Hall presumably for an avenue in 1700. Kip's engraving of Dunham Massey dated 1697 shows two established avenues together with trees in the formal gardens by the hall. The formal gardens at Cholmondeley near the old hall were laid out in 1691 and no doubt included some tree planting.

Timber Operations 17th - 18th Century

Estate timber was important for both direct use on any building projects and maintenance, and for raising estate income. Sir Peter Leicester kept accounts of the cost of building St Peter's Chapel at Tabley in 1678. Included in them were 60 trees felled for the roof of the chapel and 6 or 7 for the seat frames, worth £60, together with 60 more trees for the roof worth £10 [3].

The Arderne papers show that in 1692 at Harden Park a valuation was carried out in which 23 trees totalled £43 6s 0d, with a classification of 'may stand', 'may be fallne', or 'rottne'. Those trees were sold. The sale agreement read 'the three and twenty trees now marked and valued by George Whitby of Alvandley standing in Harden Park' and included the condition that sawpit or pits could be made in the park[4].

A notebook dated 1699 for Arley Estate gives the value of trees felled in Arley Walks. The book lists trees by number and against each one is an estimated value, and against a few the actual price obtained is noted. The tree of highest value, an oak, was sold for £7 having being valued at £6 4s 0d. The estimated value of 115 oaks totalled £260 2s 10d, and 29 ash totalled £10 11s 0d[5].

Extracts from Peter Harper's account book at Arley during the period 1758-1770 illustrate the variety of forest produce on the estate [6].

23. 3.1758	For 720 foot of windblown poplar at 6½d	£19 14s 4d
15.12.1758	For 206 foot of crooked timber from Aston Park at 9d per foot	£ 7 14s 6d
23. 5.1759	For 3 ton of willow wood	£ 1 16s 0d
14. 5.1761	For 160 alders in Aston Budworth & Crowley	£24 0s 0d
7.11.1761	For 150 birch at Sutton	1s 9d
3.7.1762	For wagon load and ½ of ash bows	18s 0d
30.11.1762	For 15 cord of wood, Appleton Moss at 7/6	£ 5 12s 6d
19.2.1763	For 3 ton 17cwt willow wood at 12d per cwt	£ 3 17s 0d
30.12.1765	For 25 cords of wood cut and cloven, ready for burning at 10/-	£17 10s 0d
	For 3 cart loads of charcoal of one dozen each, four seams over	£ 4 0s 0d
2. 4.1770	For parcel of ash fallen by Birch Brook 126 foot at 8½d	£ 4 9s 3d

There were many similar small sales at the time, but there were also some large ones. Arley Estate advertised a sizeable parcel of timber in Adams Weekly in February 1758 [7]. It read:

> A parcel of timber consisting of 1073 Oaks, fit for building Ships, Flats, or Boats together with 570 Ash all regularly marked and numbered and growing in the demesne and other lands in Sutton near Frodsham Bridge on the River Wever in the county of Chester. Attendance will be given for sale of the said timber at the house of Mr Seamen, the Eagle and Child in Warrington in the county of Lancaster on Wednesday the 22nd March next when the trees will be exposed to sale to the best bidder according to proposals to be there produced and in the mean time the said timber may be viewed by applying to Mr Thomas Hough of Sutton aforesaid.

Mr Hough was said to be the leading leaseholder in Sutton Weaver, a wealthy and elderly quaker whose family had been in Sutton since at least the 16th century, who was a friend of Sir Peter Warburton.

The timber was purchased by Messrs Garrol and Pownall who were building the 28 gun *HMS Liverpool* at the time. However they worked the timber parcel over a

11. Tree transplanting machine of the kind that may have been used for moving large lime at Arley. From *The Tree Lifter* by Colonel Greenwood, published by Longmans Green, 1876.

three year period, paying in instalments which totalled £1259 17s 3½d. There was a further sale during 1761-3 at Arley to Messrs Fisher, Golightly, and Grayson, who were also connected with naval shipbuilding in Liverpool, that fetched £1450. Bark sales were also important and a 1771 valuation of 826 trees felled on various tenements gave a bark value of £224 3s 6d. Only 385 of these trees had a timber value which totalled £154 17s 0d. This was farm timber and there was a note of use - rails, hang stumps, clump stumps, barn doors, and gate bars - so the trees were not large.

During the period 1758-1763 Sir Peter Warburton was rebuilding the hall at Arley, and no doubt timber sales went a long way towards financing the work. Large estates employed sawyers almost continuously to meet the needs of the estate and tenants for timber. The Grosvenor Estate books [8] show annual payments to John Huxley, sawyers, & partners for the period 1738-56 together with payments to others for felling and cutting up. John Williams and partners were felling, knolling, and crosscutting 170 oak trees in the park at Eaton in 1738. Mr Thomas was felling 10 oak trees in a stack yard at Burton in 1739 and felling and cutting up 66 large old oaks in the park. John Williams was also cording wood, while John Davies was burning wood for charcoal, 1170 measures in 1739 for £4 17s 6d and an unspecified quantity in 1740 for £8 15s 9d [9]. He was described as a coalman in the estate book. These rates can be compared with those at Dunham Massey which were 3d per measure in the years 1774-82 when they came down to 2d, possibly because of competition from coal.

Measures and cords may have varied between estates. Ten different cord sizes were in use in South Wales at different times in the 16th-18th centuries for charcoal.

Naval timber was always provided on a load basis, a load being 50 cubic feet. Except for sawn or squared timber accurate log measurement was not possible until Edward Hoppus compiled his *Practical Tables Made Easy* in 1736. Hoppus foot tables later became widely used in the trade for calculating the volume of round logs or trees, and continued in use until metrication in 1972. Even today they are still used by some, particularly in the hardwood trade.

Planting and Estate Forestry Practice 18th and 19th Century

The 2nd Earl of Warrington carried out considerable planting at Dunham Massey in the first half of the 18th century, which included the Langham Grove planted in memory of his mother in 1714. It is said that he planted no less than 100,000 oaks, elms, and beech and when it was suggested this was extravagant he replied:

> Gentlemen, you may think it strange that I do these things; but I have the inward satisfaction in my own breast; the benefit of posterity; and my survivors will receive more than double the profit, than by any other method I could possibly take for their interest [11].

Some idea of estate woodland practice mid 18th century is given in a survey of Sir B Broughton-Delves' lands. It was recommended in Doddington Demesne that The Rough would best be taken in hand and sown with acorns and planted with such woods as would be agreeable to the several soils. This was only a three acre wood yet there was a high degree of site selection. Oak was being directly sown and other trees planted. Checkley Wood was listed as just over 106 acres with a coppice value of 7/- per acre, amount £37 4s 4d. It was described as:

> Thinly grown with oak timber about 20 upon an acre = 2120 of nearly the size three to the ton, but in one part there is many of about a ton each. There is many parts of the land unoccupied which should be planted chiefly with sallys and alders, the whole of the underwood therein which at present is but little, having been badly abused should be cut down and then coppiced up and preserved.

This presents a picture of a wood in poor condition which was going to be taken in hand. Open areas would be planted up with willow and alder and the underwood would be cut down and coppiced, in order to get it back in good condition as coppice with standard woodland.

Chorlton Wood, listed under Steels Farm (Ralph Ravenscroft) in Chorlton Township, is recorded as just over 45 acres, but the quality of the coppice is very scrubby and valued at 2/- per acre, amount £5 12s 6d. The comment reads:

> In Chorlton Wood there is good marl in south and therefore as it is known not to produce good timber it should be fallen and cultivated which when done would be worth about 9/ per acre.

This tends to confirm the poor state much underwood and coppice was in at the time, and that certainly in one case it would be better turning it over to agriculture in 1762[12]. Economics on estates were important then as now.

The Royal Society for the Arts (RSA) gave awards to encourage the advancement of the arts, science, and industry and in 1757 forestry became eligible for the Society's awards. Firstly awards were offered for sowing acorns and planting oak, chestnut, and elm, then the list was extended to include scotch fir and Weymouth pine, being the properest sort of masts, and eventually it included seventeen species of tree useful for timber. The Society wanted to encourage tree planting for little had been done since Evelyn had published his discourse on forest trees in 1662 and the country was still acutely aware of the shortage of timber, particularly that suitable for shipbuilding. They wished to promote the planting of timber trees in the common and waste ground all over the Kingdom for the supply of the navy, the employment and advantage of the poor, as well as the ornamenting of the nation [13].

Though there had been some earlier planting, notably that at Dunham Massey, Nether Alderley, Cholmondeley, and Tatton where a poplar plantation was established in 1748 [14], it was in the period 1750-1850 that considerable areas of plantation were laid down both on newly acquired common and waste ground and on existing estate land.

Sir Peter Warburton was certainly planting at Arley by 1755 when a poplar nursery was established at Gore Farm and a further poplar nursery was planted in 1758 at Aston Park where the family were living while the hall at Arley was rebuilt. In 1759 a piece of ground in Sutton was enclosed and planted with poplar, probably situated close to the Weaver. That same year in celebration of General Wolfe's victory the Quebec Clump was planted probably with oak and Scots pine, which were ringed with 1,300 hollies. The area of this circular clump at Budworth Heath was only just over an acre, yet 21 loads of dung were used in the preparation before planting [15].

In 1756, an Act was passed 'for enclosing by mutual consent of the lords and tenants, part of any common for the purpose of planting and preserving trees fit for timber or underwood; and for more effectually preventing the unlawful destruction of trees' [16]. The freeholders in Appleton and Lymm got together in 1765 in order to enclose the commons, and Sir Peter Warburton enclosed part of his share at High Cliff to establish a plantation of just over 15 acres which was planted in 1767. This adjoined a small plantation of firs that had been planted in 1762. Edward Cook removed 2,000 young firs from the plantation on the hill in Appleton in January 1772, in order to thin them, paying 2/- per 100 trees or £10 [17]. Presumably these came from the fir plantation established in 1762. The firs are Scots pine which was also sometimes called scotch fir, or just scotch in the 18th and 19th century.

Other estates were busy planting around this period. The Stanleys of Alderley were said to have planted Scots pine on Alderley Edge in the period 1745-55 [18] and certainly in October 1798 they were felling fir on the Brindlow and in March 1799 fir timber was being hauled down from Alderley Edge [19]. The Grosvenors were establishing plantations including one at Poulton in 1755 [20], and planting trees was being carried out in the New Park at Dunham Massey at around the same time with many different species though oak was the main one [21]. There was almost certainly both larch and Scots pine included in this for the size of trees of these species blown down in a gale in 1802 suggests a planting date of 1750-1760 [22].

Sir Nicholas Ashton was awarded a gold medal by the Royal Society of the Arts for planting 133 acres of waste moorland adjoining Delamere Forest in November and December 1795. His application to the RSA dated 13th October 1800 is interesting for it describes the conditions and techniques employed and confirmed the condition Delamere Forest was in at that time. The land is productive of little more than heath, affording a scanty provision for a few sheep and rabbits. The soil is in most parts extremely thin, while under it is a great depth of sand intermixed with gravel. From old records it appears that Delamere has produced much valuable timber, so with care and proper management it should be possible to grow trees on similar waste land adjoining the forest. He enclosed the land in two lots with post and double railing. The plantations were surrounded with a ditch and white thorns were planted below the railing, and a line of French gorse was sown in a drill four feet from the fenceline. A lodge was built for one of his labourers who was ordered to devote his whole time and attention to maintaining the fences and protecting the trees from injury by sheep or otherwise.

Because of the very thin layer of vegetable soil it was considered inadvisable to plough the land. Instead the heath was burnt at the end of the summer and small stock was planted next to the surface and it was expected that they would do better than stock which was planted straight into sand from which the gravel had been screened. The latter took root quickly and the former struggled in the matted roots of the heather.

A total of 487,040 trees were planted by Archibald Dickson & Sons, nurserymen and contractors from Hassingdeanburn, near Hawick, south Scotland, 242,600 were Scots pine, 181,200 larch, 18,060 beech, 16,200 oak, 15,000 sycamore, 7,200 elm, 4,800 ash, 1,200 tree willow, 600 alder, 60 laburnum, 60 weeping birch, 30 mountain ash, and 30 sweet chestnut. The average planting distance was about 3½' x 3½'.

The planting was inspected by Archibald Dickson, the Reverend John Willan of Weaverham, and George Okell, steward for Sir Nicholas Ashton, in October 1800 who found the plantation flourishing with no more than one in twelve plants perished. In his letter to the RSA Sir Nicholas added that the flourishing state of his plantations had induced other gentlemen in the county of Chester to plant upon similar soils [23].

The land stretched south from the A556 at Sandiway, bounded on the east by Cockpit Lane and on the west by Kennel Lane. The majority of ground is now under farming or being worked for minerals, though some of the original hardwoods planted could still be standing in the belt of trees on the main road frontage.

An even larger planting scheme was carried out on J B Jodrell's estates at Taxall and Shalcross in 1795-6 on the county border near Buxton, now part of the Goyt Forest. George Small wrote to the RSA applying for an award on J B Jodrell's behalf in November 1796. 847,650 trees had been planted including 300,000 larch, 150,000 elms, 120,000 ash, 90,000 sycamore, 60,000 alder, 30,000 beech, 30,000 Scots pine, 27,000 oak together with smaller quantities of birch, mountain ash, spruce fir, silver fir, balm of gilead, and horse chestnut [24]. This was some mixture and if espacement had been similar to the scheme adjoining Delamere about 320 acres were planted. According to Marshall [25] a gentleman by the name of White contracted to find plants and to plant the whole of this land at £5 per acre it being one of the articles of agreement that half the trees planted should be firs.

Ormerod describes Taxall as:

> ... situated in a romantic and sequestered vale on the bank of the Goit, a clear and rapid trout stream which divides it from Derbyshire on the eastern side; to the west the ground rises into a range of rocky hills, planted with larches and other firs, which thrive in the more sheltered parts, but are cut by the sea breezes which sweep over the flat part of Cheshire, on the side where they are exposed to the westerly air [26].

Though the application for an RSA award was made, no reference was found to confirm one had been given. Perhaps there were problems with the initial establishment work for it was a difficult site.

In 1809, Dr William Makepeace Thackeray of Chester was awarded a gold medal for plantations, but these were situated in Denbigh and Meirionydd. Dr Thackeray was first cousin of Richard Thackeray, the father of the novelist [27].

The RSA gave their last awards for forestry in 1835, as they considered that their awards had by then achieved their objective of encouraging forest planting [28].

With the worries over naval timber supplies there was much discussion about oak. The Commissioners appointed to enquire into the situation nationally in 1792 asked the Chairman of the Quarter Sessions about the position in Cheshire. The improvements in roads and canals had helped to bring timber to the dockyards with which the county was connected which may have led to some overcutting, but Cheshire was not short of timber in any parts where it grew well. The use of oak timber in building had diminished, for deal imported at Liverpool was carried by canal to most parts of the county at small expense. Nevertheless oak was widely planted often in mixture with other species which were removed in thinning. Not much woodland had been converted to agriculture, neither had much hedgerow been grubbed up to enlarge the fields but the growth of oak in hedgerows was not generally encouraged. There were few or no oakwoods in Cheshire that were cut at stated periods in succession where young saplings were left at each cutting - the coppice with standards system, nor were there many underwoods [29].

In 1812, the Commissioners stated that they could not depend on private estates for their timber stocks were in a state of progressive elimination and would in the course of time be totally exhausted. Neither was it thought to be in the interest of individual proprietors to permit new plantations to grow to a size necessary for most naval purposes - long term plantations of hardwoods were considered uneconomic even then.

The Caldwell records for their Knowsley and Knutsford nurseries illustrate the range of species planted in the late 18th century both for ornamental and forest planting. Of the conifers Scots pine, Weymouth pine, balm of gilead, *Abies balsamea*, larch, silver fir, *Abies alba*, and spruce fir, *Picea abies*, were widely used. Ornamentals included Swedish juniper supplied to Birtles Estate in 1792, upright cypress supplied to Mr Braddock of Crosby in 1791, and white cedar exported to a Belfast nurseryman in 1795.

Broad leaved trees commonly included:- elm, lime, hornbeam, sycamore, poplar, less often beech, oak, and ash, and rarely sweet chestnut, alder, and Huntingdon willow. The elm included Cornish elm supplied to Arley in 1792 and English elm supplied that same year to Higmere. Grafted elm was supplied to Birtles in 1795 and wych elm to Mr Braddock of Crosby in 1791. Often they were just described as elm.

Detail of the poplar was sometimes given. These included Tacamaha supplied to Birtles in 1792, English poplar supplied to Higmere the same year, hardy Carolina poplar supplied to Arley in 1793, black poplar for planting on Alderley Edge in 1797, and black Italian poplar supplied to Mr Woodward in 1797.

Ornamental hardwoods included weeping willow, weeping birch, mountain ash, horse chestnut, plane, walnut, acacia, laburnum, evergreen oak, and American moss cup oak.

The quantities of forest trees supplied were generally small with 8,000 trees the largest specified order at the time. This consisted of 4,000 2ft oak and 4,000 2ft larch supplied to Henry Harvey Aston Esq of Aston, near Frodsham in November 1795 for £18. The same gentleman had received a bill for £60 10s the previous year for presumably a much larger quantity but the trees were not specified.

Caldwells supplied some much larger orders for forest trees in the first half of the 19th century. The Reverend John R Browne received 15,000 oak, 6,000 larch, 5,000 Scots pine and 4,000 spruce for Adlingon on 25th November 1828, followed in the spring on 18th February 1829 with a further 1,500 larch, 1,500 Scots pine, 700 spruce fir, and 200 oak presumably to complete the planting [30].

But this planting was on a small scale when compared to Wilbraham Egerton's requirements for the park at Tatton. During the years 1828-1834 he received just over half a million plants of which 84% were larch, 6% each Scots pine and Norway spruce, 2% silver fir, 1% each of balsam of gilead and ash. The only hardwoods in the ten year period from 1828-1837 were 6,000 ash, yet Caldwells in their 1824 catalogue showed oak, mountain ash, beech, horse chestnut, sweet chestnut, hornbeam and sycamore all priced at the 1,000 rate so they must have been able to supply them in quantity [31]. Were no hardwoods being planted or did Tatton have a nursery of its own or sow them direct into the plantation? On the Stamford Estates both oak and ash were being directly sown into plantations, and oak was also being set in nurseries in 1807 [32].

However the need for oak for shipbuilding was declining annually and conifers were faster growing and fashionable. The range of species available was increasing as the plant collectors searched the world for new, attractive trees and shrubs which could be grown commercially and popularised. It was a period when fortunes were being made from industry and trading, and new found wealth was being used to build country houses and villas, and establish policy woodlands and gardens around them.

The conifers from the American west were being introduced with David Douglas being responsible for the Douglas fir in 1827 followed by the grand fir, noble fir and Sitka spruce around 1832 all in time becoming important trees in British forestry [33], though more suited to high rainfall areas than Cheshire conditions.

In addition to the Tatton orders for forest trees 33,000 quicks were supplied in 1833 so hedges were being established on the estate at the time. Also in 1832, there were orders for 65lbs of gorse seed and 20lbs of broom seed, followed in 1833 with 120lbs of gorse and 30lbs of broom, and in 1834 with 37lbs each of gorse and broom. The price in 1833-4 was 1/- per lb for gorse and 10d for broom. These may have been used for establishing a protective edge to the plantations, or to establish game cover or a fuel supply for furze was a popular fuel source.

The Earl of Stamford received 1,000 birch transplants and 120lbs of gorse seed at Dunham Massey in March 1829 and this was most likely to be for a fox cover for many were being established at the time on large estates.

An entry in the Caldwell books for 21st January 1832, reads The Trustees of Lord de Tabley 'to planting new fox cover in Lower Peover at £8 8s per acre' but does not specify the plants or the acreage. This price for planting is slightly higher than a scheme carried out for the Trustees of the late J W Tatton Esq 'to planting 2 acres and 3 roods of land upon Baguley Hall Farm at £8 per acre' in March 1830.

Most of these covers were quite small in acreage but they contributed much to the Cheshire landscape. Not only had hunting become an important countryside pursuit, but shooting too, and it was starting to have an increasing influence on plantation design in the second half of the 19th century. Most plantations consisted of a mixture of broadleaved trees like beech, oak and sweet chestnut, which provided food for the birds, together with some conifers for cover and roosting. Pit planting was the method commonly used in establishment work. For instance at Capesthorne Estate between 1873 and 1890 holes were generally 18" x 18" x 12", and the cost of digging holes and planting varies from 3/- to 5/- per 100 [34]. Occasionally large trees were moved on estates for instant landscaping. In 1881 twelve limes which had been planted at Aston Park twenty five years before, were lifted and moved about $1^1/_2$ miles to Arley to take their place each side of the front approach. The normal method used was to lightly prune the tree before digging a trench round the main root system. The rootball formed would be undercut at about 3 feet depth and wrapped and chained before the tree was lifted out onto a large pair of wheels using a windlass system. Shafts would be attached and the tree would be trundled off to its new site [35].

The Rabbit, Grey Squirrel and other Pests

The rabbit was probably introduced into England in the 12th century and quickly became an important source of meat. Rabbits were kept for this purpose in warrens on many estates and warriners were employed to look after them, as for instance the warriner employed by Sir Edward Fitton at Gawsworth Estate. One of the rooms named in Sir Edward Fitton III's will in 1606 was a warriners chamber. Warrens were carefully maintained but around the 17th century, with increased interest in sporting, there were changes in land use, and predators on rabbits were controlled. The rabbit population quickly increased and the rabbit became a pest.

At Tillstone Heath in 1785, Thomas Davenport enclosed 12 acres of common with the permission of Lord Dysart. He planted hedges of thorn, but in the winter of 1784-5 the frost was severe and prolonged and rabbits destroyed the 4 year old quick sets by gnawing away the bark at their base. The quicks had to be cut back to ground level so that they might shoot afresh [36].

Warrens were still being established at that time, for in 1897 an area of $2^1/2$ acres was fenced off in the park at Capesthorne as a warren. Bracken was planted in the new rabbit cover in 1898 followed by alder and rhododendron. Elsewhere on the estate the tenant at Pikelow Farm, Marton was complaining about the rabbit problem and the agent, Mr Evans, noted in the estate book in April 1897, that the keepers had been asked to keep them down. That same year Oak Farm plantation at Marton was replanted and wire netting had to be used to protect the plantation from rabbits.

The Peckforton Estate Re-afforestation Diary 1921-52 notes that all the new plantations since 1922 were netted against rabbits except for poplar plants which were individually protected.

Rabbits have remained a threat. Myxomatosis, a virus, reduced the population to very low levels in the 1960's and for a time rabbit protection became unnecessary, reducing planting costs considerably. However the rabbit had been building up resistance to the disease and populations are returning to their former numbers.

Rabbit fencing is no barrier to hares who are unaffected by myxomatosis. Hares sometimes chop off leaders of young newly planted trees and leave the top lying on the ground, but they are rarely present in sufficient numbers to cause widespread damage. There is more risk when establishing plantations on agricultural ground.

The Grey Squirrel was introduced into Cheshire in 1876 by Thomas Brocklehurst to the Henbury Estate with the best of intentions. Around that time it was also introduced to a number of midland and southern counties. The grey squirrel has developed into a very serious pest, causing widespread damage to young hardwood trees and sometimes conifers, stripping off the bark and sometimes girdling the trees. Squirrels are common throughout the county in woodlands, parks, and gardens. The forester at Henbury Estate, where large groups of oak, beech, and other hardwoods have been planted to replace overmature trees, now has to pay constant attention to squirrel control, which has become standard practice in woodland management countrywide.

An itinerate herd of red deer roams the countryside along the eastern edge of Cheshire, but elsewhere in the county deer are confined to parks such as Lyme and Tatton. There is an expanding population of roe deer and muntjak in Staffordshire and Shropshire and they may yet move into Cheshire. Browsing can be a problem in young plantations.

Voles and mice can also damage young stock and eat seeds reducing the possibilities of natural regeneration. The Peckforton Woodland Diary notes damage from mice in 1927 when they were eating round ash roots in a young plantation. Damage to young trees is normally only found when sudden increases occur in the rodent population. These are usually short-lived and balance is restored by their natural predators.

Timber Operations from the 19th Century, Sawing and Sawmilling

A great storm struck Dunham Massey in 1802, blowing over some of the largest trees, and the heronry with them. A huge oak containing 373½ feet of timber was sold at 6/6d per foot for supply to Sir Robert Peel & Co as timber for a mill, while a large elm of 146 feet sold at 5/-. Included in the sale were 6334 feet of Scots pine and larch which must have been some of the first home-grown Cheshire softwood timber to go on the market selling at 1/- - 1/2d per foot [38].

Estate timber was an important asset and reserve capital. The timber sales at Arley between 1758 and 1763 occurred at a time when Sir Peter Egerton-Warburton was rebuilding the hall. A timber valuation was carried out in 1826 probably because R E Egerton-Warburton wished to know how much capital could be raised for building. He had come of age that year and George Latham had been commissioned to design a new hall. The timber was valued at £12,000 by the valuer who charged a rate of 2d per £100 for the assessment [39]. The extent of the actual sales which followed is not known, but they would certainly have helped to meet the cost of the building in 1832-5 which was approximately £13,000. It is interesting to note that the fee rate for a large timber valuation today is not very different to that applicable in 1826.

The Stamford Estate timber sales book 1825-30 for Dunham Massey gives an indication of prices obtained for timber at the stump at the time. These ranged from 1/3d per foot for alder and lime, 1/6d for poplar, 2/- for beech, 2/6d for elm and chestnut, 3/- for ash, and 3/2d - 3/6d for oak. Bark sales ranged from £8 10s to £10 10s per ton.

Timber and logs were either sawn up on site where the trees were felled or hauled in to the point of use for conversion using horse transport, or if there was good water, flotation or rafting. The latter method might have been used on the Dee, Weaver and Mersey. Canal construction in the 18th century improved transport facilities considerably in rural areas and provided easier access to many woodlands. Undoubtedly much sawn timber was transported by canal and along navigable rivers. A timber yard and docking facility covering an area of almost 3 statute acres was sited on the River Weaver just west of Frodsham Bridge in 1754 [40] and there must have been others.

It was normal to make allowances for pitsawying in timber sale agreements. William Wright purchased some timber from the Marquess of Cholmondeley in 1819. The agreement allowed for

> servants, workmen, and assignees with horses, waggons, parts, carriages, and proper machines, utensils and implements and to fell, cut down, or scrub up the roots the said trees and wood and for the purpose of stub cutting, sawying, squaring, and converting and working up the same[41].

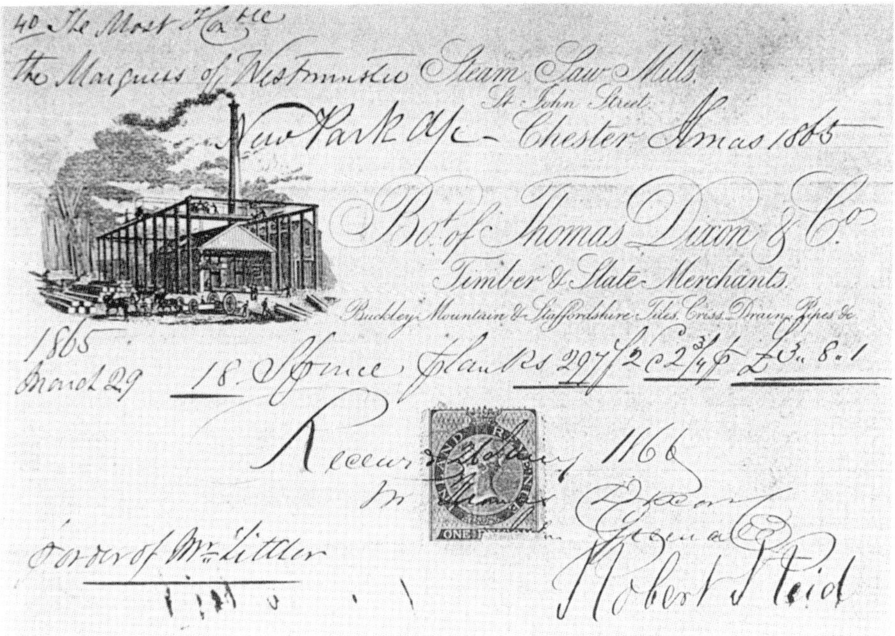
Steam Saw Mills.
St. John Street.
Chester
Bot. of Thomas Dixon & Co.
Timber & Slate Merchants.
Buckley Mountain & Staffordshire Tiles, Cross Drain Pipes &c.
1865
18 Spruce Planks
£3.8.1
Order of Mr. Littler

12. A typical steam mill is illustrated on this 1865 invoice for spruce planks from timber merchants Thomas Dixon & Co, Chester. From the Eaton Estate Papers, 59/15/2.

The agreement gave 'the liberty to make sawpits, pitsheads, and cabins' which had to be filled and levelled on completion.

In pitsawying the log is placed longitudinally over a deep pit and supported on wooden rollers. Two men operate the rip saw, the top sawyer standing on the log and the pitman in the pit beneath it. The top sawyer has the heavier job for he has to raise the saw for every stroke but the pitman receives a continual shower of sawdust to compensate. It was easier to cleave or hew timber into shape if that was possible. Most estate yards had a sawpit.

The earliest industrial sawmills were erected on the continent in the 16th century but there was considerable resistance from pitsawyers to any introduction in this country, for they feared it would effect their trade. However the Royal Society for the Arts was concerned that large quantities of timber were being sawn by foreign labour, and they offered a prize of £100 to the person who should first erect a good sawmill and work it for one year [42]. The prize was claimed by John Stansfield for a sawmill at Bingley in Yorkshire in 1761, with a water wheel supplying the power of three frame saws [43]. Dingley was awarded a gold medal by the RSA in 1767 for a sawmill in Limehouse, London. A committee reported that it worked well and was advantageously sited for river and canal transport. His mill was wind driven and could operate up to 30 saws in a gale. The following year the mill was badly damaged by disgruntled sawyers fearing for their livelihoods and Parliament compensated Dingley with £2,000.

The sawmill had a slow and difficult start and it was the 19th century before milling became established in Cheshire, driven by water or steam. Most of these were commercial enterprises using both imported and homegrown timber, such as Dixon's steam mill in Chester. However a sawmill was established on the banks of the Weaver in 1852 on the site of an old ironworks where iron plates had been made out of scrap iron, flattened by a large water driven hammer. This sawmill was making soap boxes from Scots pine supplied entirely from the Delamere Forest [44]. Another mill operational near Delamere towards the end of the 19th century was the steam sawmill at Cuddington which was hoping to get supplies of oak and pine from the forest in 1895.

Some estates decided to set up sawmills with Dunham Massey taking the lead in around 1860 when the old cornmill close to the hall was converted and fitted out with a framesaw and circular saw, which were water driven. It did not operate for long for it was in disuse by 1895, probably because so much water was used to operate the saws that the lake would be emptied [45]. However the sawmill has since been restored by the National Trust.

A water driven sawmill was established at Capesthorne Estate by 1877 and was operational until well into the 20th century. Under permanent improvements listed in Mr John Shaw's report of 1885-93 dated 16th October 1883 he records £17 15s being spent on new pumps in 1888, and gives an estimated cost of £87 19s for renovating the machinery and partial re-roofing, stating that the work was urgent as the machinery was in a dangerous state. Later monthly reports noted repairs and new roof and skylights in 1897, edging and cleaning up the drive from the sawmill to the bridge over the pool in 1898, and new soling and waterbuckets to waterwheel in 1900 [46]. There is little left of the mill now but the building, which is used by a boat repairer. A second sawmill was established by the estate in agricultural buildings close to the A34 Congleton road early this century powered by steam, and later by electricity. The two sawyers who worked in this mill just before the Second World War lived quite close to each other near Congleton but between them they could only afford to buy one bicycle to get to work every day. They took the nine mile journey in turns, one cycling 1½ miles the other walking 1½ miles, the cycle being left in the hedge for the other to pick up, then turn about.

Mr George Ridley, who started work at the Eaton Estate as a pupil forester in 1926, recalls that the steam engine which powered the sawmill at Belgrave was kept in immaculate condition. The sawbenches were operated by the Wainwright brothers. Billie and Tommy rode in from Old Bretton every day sporting billycock hats which they changed for cloth caps for work. The Wainwrights also operated the light railway which linked Balderton Station with Eaton Hall. Though its main purpose was to bring in a load of coal every fortnight, there was a link to the sawmill so that the timber could be transported from time to time. The sawmill in 1932 consisted of a rack bench and breast bench driven by steam, and a petrol driven crosscut. The circular saws in use were the inserted tooth type, and round logs up to a diameter of 30 inches could be sawn. There was also a pressure tank for creosoting fence material. This may have been in use for some years for creosoted beech timber was noted to be in good condition twenty years after the treatment [47]. In 1944, an additional sawmill was erected at Balderton Station, where two circular saws and a conveyor were installed to log firewood which was railed to Manchester. Because of the great age of many of the trees growing in open situations on the estate, there were large quantities of over mature timber with heavy crowns. The Manchester firewood market proved an excellent outlet for low grade material until smokeless zones were created. The Belgrave mill converted all the better quality logs.

The steam engine which powered the Belgrave sawmill became redundant in 1950 when the mill was re-equipped. Pulford Estates, a management and contracting company, had been established to service the woodlands on Grosvenor estates throughout Britain. The new Pulford sawmill converted hardwoods and mining timber. An electrically powered bandmill had been installed equipped with Guillet saws. Timber came in from many estates including Pale near Bala, and the Bridgewater Estate near Ellesmere. It operated until 1965 when it was moved to the site now used by Jacksons Fencing and re-equipped with Stenner saws. The old site is now occupied by the Grosvenor Garden Centre, and if you go there see if you can spot the old engine shed, the older building with a large window straight in front immediately you turn off the main road. The Stenner equipped mill closed in 1968 when the Pulford business closed down.

Other estates including Peckforton, Tatton and Cholmondeley also operated sawmills this century, but only the Cholmondeley Estate mill remains active.

There was much felling in World War I to meet national requirements, and Peckforton was one of the main estates affected. Again in the Second World War there were national needs and a further spate of felling occurred which included 342 acres clear felled at Delamere Forest. On the Eaton Estate fellings included Kennel Wood, Bretton Drive, and the River Rides where there were very fine large beech, while there was a massive clearance operation in the deer park where the RAF aerodrome was built in 1942. There, all the old park trees, mainly oak, had to be felled and uprooted before the runways could be built. Not far from the end of the runway stood a fine Cedar of Lebanon which the Air Ministry wished to fell for

13. Oak timber leaving the Grosvenor Estate in 1950. Nearest the camera is Mr Laurie Adams, now a well known timber merchant.

14. Cedar of Lebanon topped in 1942 to give a clearer flightpath to the wartime airfield at Eaton Park

safety reasons as it was close to the flightpath. The Duke said no, and as a compromise solution the tree had its top removed at about 40 feet, and the tree stands proudly there today.

Estate forestry from the end of the 19th century

New interest in forestry in the county was generated in 1896 when the English Aboricultural Society held their 15th annual meeting in Chester. Besides the visit to Dickson's nursery described in the previous chapter, there were visits the following day to Eaton and Hawarden Estates both by then noted for their aboriculture and plantations. Evidently there were noteworthy specimen trees at Eaton including Atlantic cedars containing about 100 feet of timber each, cedars of Lebanon, cut-leaved beech, manna ash, and three 45 feet high swamp cypress. Mention was made of the old oaks at the stud, two of which featured in the George Stubbs oil painting of about 1766. The local committee at the time chaired by Alderman G A Dickson drew up the programme. Committee members also included Mr A T Gillander of Knutsford, Mr W Elder of Cholmondeley Park, Mr E J Baillie of Upton and Mr W A Forster, the secretary, of Belgrave Lodge, Pulford [48].

Four years later the Society held its annual meeting in Manchester, visiting Clibrans nurseries at Hale, and then Dunham Massey. The party admired a cork oak planted in 1833 by the 6th Earl of Stamford, and some very large beech near the orangery including one of 16' 9" girth containing 350 feet of timber. Unfortunately, the largest of the tulip trees, 150 years old, had been killed by lightning in a summer storm the year before and two others had been similarly killed in 1896 and 1898. They were said to be some of the largest tulip trees to be found in the country [49].

The Society provided a valuable meeting point where woodland owners and their agents could get together to recount their experiences and exchange ideas on techniques, for there was no state guidance, research, or assistance such as was already provided in some European countries. Insufficient knowledge had led to many mistakes in species selection and growing techniques.

As the first report of the Forestry Commission stated in 1920:

> it is easy to criticise British private forestry, but it must not be forgotten that it has at least three solid achievements to its credit which far outweigh the minor errors which have marked some stages of its progress.
>
> 1. The trees were planted, which during the recent war when it was a choice between importing food or timber, enabled the people of these islands to be fed.
>
> 2. The faster growing conifers were introduced and the way paved for planting them on a commercial scale, a step which may, if there is no

unforseen setback, revolutionise continental ideas on length of rotation and maximum yield.

3. Experiments were made which, though not fully recorded, should, with intelligent investigation, supply much of the information required for the successful establishment of State forests.

Following the first war, a start was made with the replanting of felled areas, as for instance on the Peckforton Estate[50] where a re-afforestation programme was commenced in 1921. There was extensive planting in Gregory's Wood, Sheens Rough, Pennsylvania Wood, Stanners Nab, and Waste Hill Wood between 1922 and 1926. The new plantations included 13 acres of black Italian poplar planted at 15 feet espacement and 5 acres of a mixture of ash and European larch, and areas of Douglas fir in Gregory's Wood, 30 acres of a mixture of 2 sweet chestnut to 1 ash in Pennsylvania Wood, 30 acres of sitka spruce in Waste Hill, together with areas of Scots and Corsican pines in Stanners Nab. Thus there was wide variety in the plantings. 212½ acres were planted between 1922 and 1927 on the Peckforton Estate.

At the nearby Bolesworth Estate on the Bickerton Hills towards Gallantry Bank and close to the Sandstone Trail, Tower Wood and New Plantation were both planted just before the war in 1913 with Scots and Corsican pine, while Barnhill, Lower Rawhead, and large parts of Cawleys and Bodnick Wood were planted just after the war in 1920 and 1921. Though the sandstones with their acid soils would naturally be clothed in sessile oak woodland of which there are several extensive blocks, pine grows well in the conditions producing good timber yet fitting into the sandstone landscape of the hills as if it had always been there.

Though the Forestry Commission was established in 1919, it was many years before the benefits of its research and advisory work were fully appreciated by woodland owners, for the country was moving into a state of economic depression and woodland work was frequently neglected between the wars. The Commission attempted to encourage planting and offered grants which included £2 per acre for softwood planting and £4 per acre for hardwoods in 1927 but this had little effect [51].

Woodlands providing sporting facilities, shelter, and attractive scenery continued to be more important to the Cheshire landowner than those which produced timber alone. Mixed woodland of hardwoods and conifers were favoured. Despite the prevailing economic conditions there were large staff lists on the main estates. When Mr George Ridley started work as a pupil forester at Eaton in 1926 there were 82 men on the forestry payroll.

At the time there were 32 miles of drives to be maintained, all the hedges to be cut, parkland trees and amenity woodland to be cared for, while the hay had to be harvested as that was a forestry responsibility, and four or five men were permanently employed in the sawmill. The men worked under the Head Forester, Mr Myles, who had joined the Duke of Westminster's staff in 1910. Like many early foresters on the great estates he was a Scot, for estate forestry had developed to a much greater extent in Scotland.

There were often conflicts of interest between the game and forest departments on estates, but not so at Eaton where Mr Myles combined the duties of the head forester and head gamekeeper. He worked on through the years of the Second World War before retiring, when Peter Barnie, another Scot, came to Eaton from the Penrhyn Castle Estate to take over.

Estate staff were depleted during the war when little work was carried out except felling to meet national needs. At Peckforton Estate there was no timber available because of the extensive felling in the first war and thinning operations were discontinued in view of the danger of brash catching fire from incendiary bombs [52]. As at the Eaton Estate, there were considerable fellings of park trees at Tatton to accommodate an airfield and dropping zone for parachutists.

Because of extensive felling in the two world wars and the long period of low activity in the years between, the forest resource both nationally and locally in Cheshire was depleted, and much needed to be done to rehabilitate devastated and neglected woodlands. It was during this period that many of the remaining coppice woodlands fell into neglect, never to recover. Some were later converted into plantations as improved grants became available after the war through the Forestry Commission Dedication Scheme instituted in 1947, and the approved woods and small woods scheme which started in 1953 and ran until 1962.

Just after the war, Grosvenor Estates, who by then had George Ridley as their Chief Agent, acquired a number of properties throughout Britain with considerable forest interests. As mentioned earlier in this chapter a management and contracting company, Pulford Estates, was established in 1949 both to operate these woodlands and to provide forestry services to others. Among its Directors were Eric Isherwood and Langshaw Rowland who had been running the sawmills and timber production work at Eaton on a contract basis. Both were well-known in forestry circles. Eric Isherwood was one of the Isherwood family of Wem, renowned sawmillers dealing largely with quality hardwoods such as oak and ash. Langshaw Rowland was an experienced forester who later took high office in the Royal Forestry Society (formerly the Royal English Aboricultural Society). He was President of the Society from 1958-60.

Following the war, there was urgent need for more trained foresters nationally to supervise the rapid expansion of forest activity, and in 1949 shortly after Peter Barnie came to Eaton it was decided to open a forestry training school and utilise some of the old RAF buildings on the aerodrome. Much of the teaching was done by estate staff and practical experience was obtained in the estate woodlands. There was close liaison with the Forestry Commission and trainees were taken to Woodmans and Forester certificate standard. Some well-known foresters received their initial training at Eaton, including the Cheshire County Forestry Officer, Robert Price. Nationally the need for training places decreased in the sixties and the school closed down.

Over the last forty years estate woodlands have been rehabilitated and brought back into management, helped to some extent by fiscal incentives and grants. The majority of replanting was carried out with the object of producing a final crop of hardwoods, normally oak on the heavier soils and beech on the light soils, nursed up by pine or larch or occasionally spruce which is gradually removed in thinning. The conifers provide some intermediate revenue to help finance the long-term crops of hardwood of 100 years or more, and they also give shelter and cover to game and wildlife particularly in the winter.

There have been setbacks, some caused by changes in taxation and forest policy which have lead to a reduction of the forest workforce and consequently woodland maintenance, others due to natural causes. The drought of 1976, followed by more recent drought years led to decline and sometimes loss of many fine old beech and to some extent other hardwoods. Most evident though, was the loss of almost all the mature elm in the county through the ravages of Dutch elm disease in the seventies. Spread by the elm bark beetle, the fungus chokes the vessels of the tree resulting in sudden and rapid death. Fortunately elm regenerates by root suckers and there is now some sign of recovery, possibly because the fungus is less virulent or the beetle population is now very low.

Despite the setbacks the standard of woodland management has consistently improved, aided by the flow of research information from the Forestry Commission and others. Organisations like Timber Growers United Kingdom which represents woodland owners, the Royal Forestry Society which anyone interested in trees and woodland can join, and the Country Landowners Association have helped to disseminate information and keep their members up with changing times. The Institute of Chartered Foresters is the representative body of the forestry profession, which has the maintenance and improvement of standards of practice and understanding of forestry, as one of its principal objectives.

Unfortunately many small woods still lie neglected, sometimes because of the cost of improvements, sometimes because of lack of time or knowledge. Many have difficult access and contain little marketable timber to pay for rehabilitation despite the grants available. These woods are vital in a landscape and wildlife context, and deserve attention and care.

Chapter 9 - Delamere and Macclesfield Forests from the 19th Century Onwards

Long before the 19th century, Macclesfield Forest was alienated from the Crown and wooded parts of the forest were taken over by many different owners. However Delamere was still a Royal Forest and came under the control of the Surveyor General of Crown Lands.

Towards the end of the 18th century the government realised that the country's timber supplies were dangerously low and there was insufficient oak available for shipbuilding. A commission of inquiry was set up in 1786 to investigate the situation. Royal forests until that time had been used for hunting and meeting the needs of rightholders rather than managed with the object of producing timber. Holland in his report on Cheshire agriculture in 1808 described Delamere as 'heath affording a scanty subsistence to a few sheep and rabbits' rather than forest [1].

A Department of Woods, Forests, and Land Revenue took control of the Royal Forests and set out to plan the nation's timber supplies and convert the Royal forests, including Delamere, to timber production. The findings and proposals were published in 1812 in the first report that the Commissioners of His Majesty's Woods, Forests, and Land Revenue produced [2]. In this report they calculated that 100,000 acres of forest would be needed to provide the annual requirement of naval timber for shipbuilding and maintenance. This was based on a 100 year rotation for oak, with annual felling and replanting programme of 1000 acres yielding 110,000 loads or 165,000 tons of timber annually.

The Commissioners assumed that all the royal forests were suited to oak timber production, and an Act to enclose Delamere received the Royal Assent in June 1812[3]. The act estimated the open forest area to be about 8,000 acres and the Old Pale and New Pale enclosures to be about 750 acres. The Commissioners were asked to divide the forest area between the Crown who would have exclusive use of its moiety with all rights extinguished, and Rightholders. There was much argument and negotiation over the settlement of claims, further legislation was required and it was 1820 before the final award was made. There was concern about rabbits and the legislation stated that no rabbits were to be kept on any part of the forest allotted.

The Crown was finally left with a forest area of 3,847 acres after 191 acres had been set aside for church allotments and isolated areas totalling 58 acres had been sold off.

The Commissioners immediately embarked on a considerable planting programme after the forest was fenced. 1,000 acres had been planted by 1816, 2,313 acres by 1819, and 3,647 acres by 1823, just ten years from commencement which was no mean achievement. The main species planted was Pedunculate oak though Sessile oak was the main component of the natural forest before it was denuded.

Growing techniques had been discussed in the Commissioners first report in 1812 when the views of experienced growers and nurserymen were sought. By the time of the second report in 1816 some experience had been gained in the use of oak. In the first plantings a mixture of direct sown acorns and oak seedlings was used in most instances. Heavy losses occurred in the acorns, many of which were destroyed by birds, mice, and other vermin, while those germinating had to compete with high grass and fern. By then nurseries had been established in the many Royal forests to provide stock for remaining planting and loss replacement. Delamere is not mentioned by name in the report, but it is very probable that by 1816 it had a nursery and similar planting techniques to those described had been used, though the remarks refer to the Royal forests collectively [4].

It is not thought that areas were ploughed before planting, but an extensive drainage system was established at commencement.

Early Difficulties

The first suggestion that there might be a problem with the oak was given in the Commissioners 1823 report [5] where they expressed disappointment with the oaks in Delamere but stated that more time was needed. This report noted an alteration in planting method. In all but the most sheltered situations a mixture of firs had been planted with the oak from 1820 on. There were local objections to planting firs at Delamere, but the Commissioners stood firm on their new technique. The report states 'We have no doubt whatever in our minds of the great benefit which will be derived by mixing firs with oaks in all future enclosures and plantations, but in doing so the most watchful attention will be required to thin out the firs before they outgrow the oak or draw them up to a height disproportionate to the strength of the stem'. Thinnings in early years should be carried out without regard to the value of the produce which for a few years would probably not defray expenses.

There was again a cautionary note in the 1826 report [6], though this was not specific to Delamere. It stated that there were differences in site and there were some areas where the young oak had not grown as well as expected, but by using other trees like firs and beech in mixture, the oaks will ultimately succeed. Sweet chestnut had been used to a small extent at Delamere.

Though there had been some returns from thinning, Delamere Forest was still not producing net income by 1849. When a new Commissioner, Mr Kennedy, was appointed in 1851 he saw a need to improve management and increase returns from the forest. He called in a Consultant, James Brown, who was an experienced

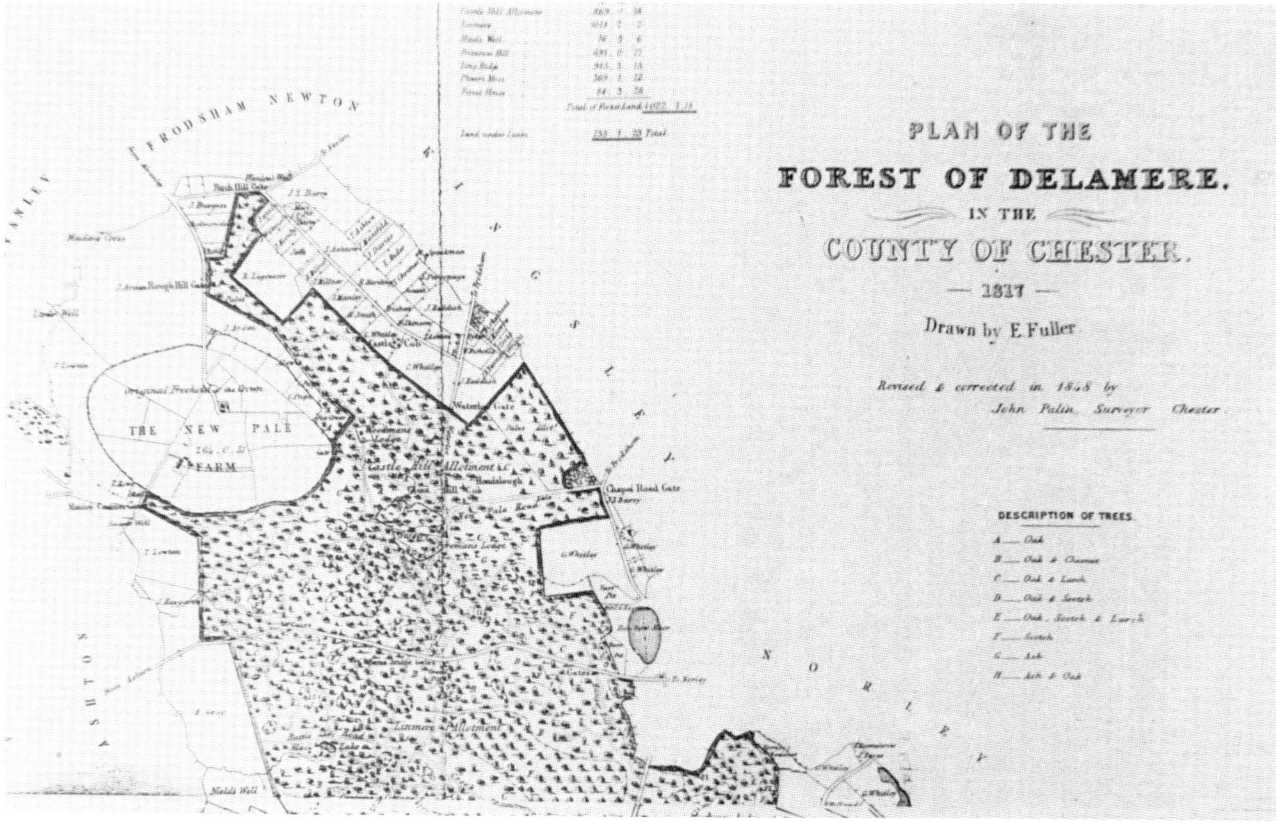

15. Part of Delamere Forest from the 1817 map by E Fuller, revised by Chester surveyor John Palin in 1848.

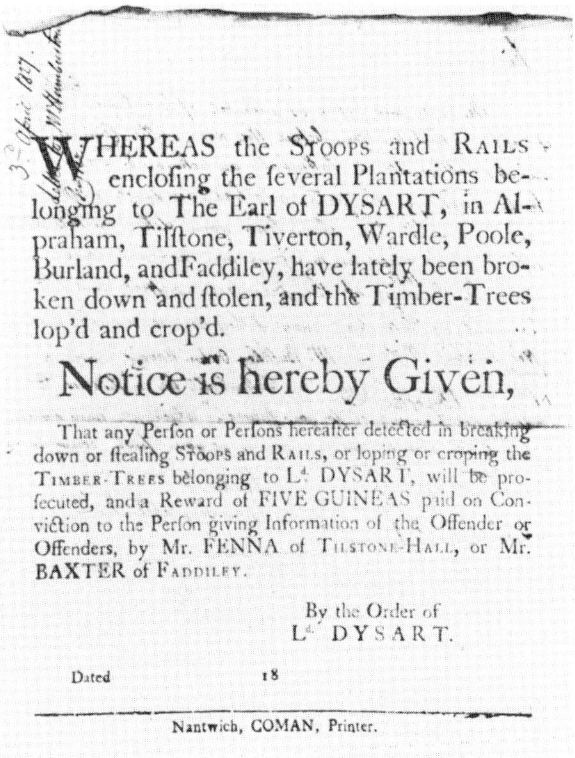

WHEREAS the STOOPS and RAILS encloſing the ſeveral Plantations belonging to The Earl of DYSART, in Alpraham, Tilſtone, Tiverton, Wardle, Poole, Burland, and Faddiley, have lately been broken down and ſtolen, and the Timber-Trees lop'd and crop'd.

Notice is hereby Given,

That any Perſon or Perſons hereafter detected in breaking down or ſtealing STOOPS and RAILS, or loping or croping the TIMBER-TREES belonging to L^d. DYSART, will be proſecuted, and a Reward of FIVE GUINEAS paid on Conviction to the Perſon giving Information of the Offender or Offenders, by Mr. FENNA of TILSTONE-HALL, or Mr. BAXTER of FADDILEY.

By the Order of
L^d. DYSART.

Dated 18

Nantwich, COMAN, Printer.

16. Earl of Dysart's warning notice, c. 1827.
Cheshire CRO DCR13/14

Scottish forester, to survey and report on the situation in 1852 [7]. James Brown was the author of a well-known book on forestry, 'The Forester', published in 1847.

After carrying out his field work James Brown submitted a detailed report in which he advocated a regular thinning programme in order to improve the quality of the crop, condemning the close growing stands of trees. He divided the forest into five land categories in each of the seven forest allotments[8]. The categories were as follows:-

> First - Good dry loamy land at present under a crop of oak, chestnut, and larch at wide distances and about 30 years od, in a fair and promising state totalling 700 acres.
>
> Second - Good dry loamy land at present under a crop of Scots pine and larch at wide distances and about 30 years old intermixed with oak and chestnut plants under 20 years of age and capable of growing these to valuable dimensions, totalling 700 acres.

Third - Poor thin moorish land, at present under a crop of the same description as the second category, but which is not capable of growing hardwood to valuable size, totalling 700 acres.

Fourth - Pure moss land at present under a crop of Scots pine with a few patches of alder and birch, totalling 380 acres.

Fifth - Moorish land under a crop of Scots pine only, totalling 364 acres.

In the first two categories he recommended favouring oak and removing Scots pine and larch, and in category three the hardwoods should be cleared and the ground replanted with Scots pine at the rate of 100 acres per year. In category four the pine was far too close and should be thinned out to a seven foot espacement, and the ash planted on Great Blackmere and Linmere mosses was failing and should be cleared and replanted with pine. In category five the replanting of the 100 acres of burnt ground in Plovers Moss should be completed with Scots pine, and the pine crop on the remainder needed to be thinned.

He made the general recommendation that the whole forest should be regularly thinned every five years, and in order to make this practicable the forest should be divided into five equal parts and one part should be thinned each year.

Brown produced a financial forecast which summarised annual expenditure and income for the period 1852-71 with quinquennial valuations of the standing crop, and a detailed estimate for the first year 1852-3. The latter increased the revenue and decreased expenditure in the budget previously prepared by the Deputy Surveyor of the forest Mr Lipscomb. The workforce requirement was assessed as 40 exclusive of the foreman for the first five years, and 30 from then on. In the budget for 1852-3 there was an allowance for the deputy surveyor, foreman, and four woodmen. The deputy surveyor would receive inclusive of allowances £228 17s 5d, foreman £54 12s 0d, and woodmen £33 3s 0d each, while there was provision of £800 for day labour and £600 for piecework over the year.

Brown's report confirmed much of the criticism that had appeared in both the technical and daily press about the management and methods employed at Delamere. His report was very well received by Commissioner Kennedy who put it into effect and gave Mr Lipscomb, the Deputy Surveyor, his notice for he had not held him in high regard. However others were critical of Brown looking on him as a Scot lacking experience of English conditions, hardwoods, and naval timber. There were persistent reports of mismanagement, and in 1854 shortly after Brown had completed his report, Parliament again looked at the position of the Royal forests as a whole and a Select Committee was appointed.

Meanwhile the Treasury had continued to pay William Lipscomb and later in 1854 they appointed Messrs Mathews, Murton and Menzies to examine the question of the Royal forests. Commissioner Kenedy had appointed Brown to report on Delamere and other Royal forests without any reference to the Treasury. There were all the makings of a first class row. Mathews and Murton were land surveyors from Birmingham and Kent respectively, and Menzies was a Scot who held the post of Deputy Surveyor of Windsor Forest.

1854 Select Committee Evidence and Report

Deputy Surveyor Lipscomb made a number of points about his forest management. He had planted larch and Scots pine where there was heath, and oak where there was bracken [9]. The mosses had been well drained and planted with pine which at 30 years of age was becoming suitable for pit props [10]. He had been constantly planting wherever a thinning took place and where pine had improved the ground oak was planted [11]. When asked if he imagined the Act of Parliament to be so stringent that when oaks do not get higher than this table after so many years growth it prevents you grubbing them up and planting something else, he replied 'not exactly so: but my orders from the Commissioners were to press in oak wherever we could possibly get them to grow'[12].

Edwin Corbett Esq who lived near Delamere gave evidence. He thought that the management of the forest had been bad at the beginning for there had been so much pine planted that it overcrowded other trees with the result that the oak and larch are entirely cleared, and a great part of the forest has been replanted. At one time they cut racks in the pine ten yards apart and planted oak in them so that rows are ten yards apart with oak at five feet espacement within them [13].

He suggested that the reason for heavy losses in the young trees was due to spring planting and the use of large plants, and cited the case of Sir Nicholas Ashton's planting in 1795 on an area adjacent to the forest where two year old seedlings had been planted very successfully merely by the spade [14]. The 1849 Select Committee had heard that it was normal for plants to be purchased as seedlings and grown on in Delamere Nursery before planting out [15].

A severe fire had occurred around 1850 when nearly 100 acres of plantation at Plovers Moss had been destroyed. Four constables of the Cheshire Constabulary were then employed to protect the forest against intruders and cattle, for in addition to the danger of fire, encroachment was always a problem. The constables were reduced to two in 1854[16].

He described serious squirrel damage in Sir Philip Egerton's plantation close to the forest where so many trees had been bitten at the top and killed, that the plantation had been grubbed up as it would not be profitable [17]. This was the red squirrel for the grey squirrels had not been introduced into the country at that time, and a most unusual occurrence for unlike the grey squirrel which is often devastating, the red squirrel rarely damages trees.

Col William Tomkinson who had lived near Delamere for 26 years also gave evidence. He too was very critical of the management and methods adopted, particularly in connection with timber sales. Logs were drawn up into heaps in the rides, and bid for either by the measure or by the heap, so many trees or so much per foot. There was much drunkenness and irregularity amongst the men when they were selling material [18]. Apparently it was the custom for timber merchants to bring a load of ale from the Abbey Arms with the timber carriage whenever they came to buy timber [19].

The referees appointed by the Treasury also reported and were highly critical of Delamere, but they exonerated the Deputy Surveyor Lipscomb from any blame. They conclude that Delamere was in every respect unsuited to the growth of oak and that such a crop should never have been planted [20]. They could in no way approve of the management. Trees were planted in such sizes and places as to preclude any chance of success. Thinnings were expensively conducted generally over the whole forest every year instead of at intervals. Felling was unskilful, fencing was bad. Thriving larch rapidly approaching the size of good timber had been felled to give room to stunted thriftless oaks.

The referees recommended that the forest should be divided into three parts. The first, the lowlands and mosses now planted with Scots pine, should be exclusively appropriated to that crop. The second part, comprising the western portion of the Linmere allotment (part of Browns category one land) is too valuable at present to justify its destruction, and it should remain in its present state and be managed with the greatest care. The third part comprising the remainder of the entire forest should be cleared and planted with larch as a permanent crop.

Both their report and evidence given to the Committee by J Clutton Esq referred to a very severe and early snowstorm in November 1852 which caused untold havoc, breaking a vast number of oak trees as it occurred before the fall of the leaf [21].

On the 18th July 1854 the select committee made its report. The condition of Delamere was most unsatisfactory, the soil being very variable and in a large portion of the forest poor and unproductive. Nor had the management been judicious, and it appears to have been in the hands of persons incompetent for the duty [22]. In regard to Commissioner Kennedy they stated that though his proceedings may be open to objection, he evinced much zeal, energy, and vigilance in the execution of his office[23].

A major change in policy became inevitable as a result, and in 1856 the clause in the 1812 Enclosure Act which stated that the crown allotments shall forever thereafter be made and kept as nurseries for wood and timber only, and for no other use, extent or purpose whatsoever, was repealed.

Consequently approximately 1,600 acres were taken out of the forest and reclaimed to agriculture [24]. An extensive clearance and marling operation was carried out in 1860-63. A system of semi-permanent trackways was laid out so that wagon loads of marl could be brought in by locomotive. Final distribution was by horse drawn wagon over movable trackway. No doubt timber produce from the clearance was used to support the trackways. As far back as 1849 it had been reported that advantages had been taken of the market for the temporary railway sleepers and pitprops for collieries to boost revenue [25].

Conditions and Life in the Forest

In 1858 Mr Linnell took over responsibility for the forest from Mr Lipscomb and lived at Rangers Lodge, which was approached by an avenue of firs a mile and a half long. His wife, Mrs Linnell, described life in the forest in a letter to her son in Australia probably written about 1875. Life was not easy to start with and there were troublemakers. The former surveyor had not been able to control the people who continually tried to get possession of the whole place. There were threats, her windows had been riddled with shot, and the foreman's pig had been killed. Six policemen from London paraded the forest day and night, besides forest men, four woodmen, and the foreman. Theft and lawlessness in the 19th century was a problem in the woodlands as the Earl of Dysart's warning notice shows.

There was at one time a plentiful supply of blackgame, but it disappeared when the railway was built (it opened in 1869). It was not considered a good thing to have game in quantity in the forest; people came from Manchester to a private estate adjoining the forest, fifty in a gang. They jeered the keepers for not feeding the pheasants and sometimes gave a parting shot.

Mrs Linnell came to love the forest and wrote romantically about it.

> The bracken which covered the ground was six or seven feet high and in the moonlight there was a silver sheen on it which was quite enchanting. There were 21 different sorts of ferns growing there and rare bog plants and birds.
>
> There were the forest races in the forest, when the members sported their new coats, the military uniforms and the ladies blazing with their jewels were a sight to remember.

Sometimes the Linnells were roused from their sleep by a flute which a friend of the Rector's carried and played when searching barefoot for bog plants and rare fungi. Her husband is buried at Delamere Churchyard under the registered name of Forester Linnell.

An Officer of Woods report dated November 1907 states that in the period 1859 - 67 and for many years after, practically no work was done in the remaining woods except to sell timber as demand for it occurred.

In 1890 the forest was said to have consisted of over mature oak of low stocking

Plate 1. The Apostles, sycamore on glebe land at Malpas.

Plate 2. Fluted hornbeam, the Wilderness, Adlington.

Plate 3. Lime avenue at Adlington Hall, planted 1688.

Plate 4. Semi natural ancient woodland, Wheatfield Clough, Bosley. [Photo R Smart]

Plate 5. Ancient yew by path, St Lukes, Goostrey.

Plate 6. Native black poplar by the lane, Sealand Church.

Plate 7. The pleached lime avenue, Arley Hall, planted 1851.

Plate 8. Old tulip tree on the Green at Arley with young replacement

Plate 9. The Marton oak, by far the largest of Cheshire's ancient trees.

Plate 10. Recreational use of the forest, the East Trail, Delamere.

Plate 11. Scene at Jodrell Bank Arboretum.

Plate 12. Dr Hugh McAllister, Deputy Director, Ness Gardens, by the maturing pin oak.

Plate 13. Queens Park, Crewe, 1992 - to be compared with the scene in 1888 on page 91.

Plate 14. Oak on Arley Green with hollow barred to children. [Photo R Smart]

Plate 15. The use of Macclesfield Forest timber - fine old carved oak post, Adlington Hall.

Plate 16. Use of oak timber - Little Moreton Hall. [Illustrated London News Picture Library]

Plate 17. The value of farm woodland in the landscape - Gorstella Farm, near Chester.

Plate 18. The same woodland provides shelter and cover for wildlife.

Plate 19. Ancient oak by the Mere at Combermere Abbey.

and poor quality with much shake, and some Scots pine. The practice of selecting the best trees for felling had left little oak of value. The pine was generally of good quality, but on the lowlands insect pest damage and natural adverse factors reduced the quality considerably [26].

An 1892 letter to the Chronicle suggested Delamere should at some future time become as Epping Forest is to London. It complained about the ruthless felling of the beautiful avenue of dark fir nearly a mile long leading from White Lodge, Eddisbury to Eddisbury House [27].

A New Management Era Begins

In about 1892 it was decided to make the effort to restock the area of about 2,100 acres still under timber. In November that year Mr Holland advocated the drawing up of a detailed working plan such as had been done for the crown land at Windsor by Dr Schlick, Professor of Forestry at Coopers Hill College. It would impose discipline on management. He advocated the division of the forest into compartments and said that attention should be given to the way produce was sold. Auction should be tried [28].

A compartment map was drawn up and in 1893 Spencer Gore of Smith & Gore provided compartment descriptions and recommendations. The possibility of planting Corsican pine was first discussed in 1893 and it was tried the following season [29]. Estimates were prepared for planting 50 acres in autumn 1893 as follows:-

Operation	10 Ac	10 Ac	10 Ac	20 Ac
Cost of plants	£40	£30	£40	£80
Digging/Planting and Cartage	£50	£55	£50	£105
Fencing & Wirenetting	£30	£22	£22	£40
Ditching		£5		
	£120	£112	£112	£225
Value of timber on area	£40	£100	£100	£100
Net costs	£80	£12	£12	£125

It is to be noted that wire netting was required for protection against rabbits [30]. Plants used were Scots pine, Corsican pine, larch, and birch, the stock coming from Fell of Hexham and Dicksons of Chester [31].

When clearance for replanting started in 1894 scattered oak, pine, rowan, and other hardwoods were left standing to provide shelter for the young crop. In 1899 it was decided to discontinue planting larch as it was not doing well. Half the area to be planted would be Scots pine, a quarter Corsican pine, and a quarter Weymouth pine [32]. From 1900 Corsican pine was most favoured for the high dry areas, where subsequent losses were replaced with Scots and Weymouth pines.

The Manchester Guardian contained an article on Delamere on 14th June 1900 which dispelled the rumour about felling the forest, pointing out that Weymouth, Corsican, and Scots pines are taking the place of less robust trees, for the forest even then was much used by the public. Thousands of delighted townsfolk lose themselves in its pathless shades every summer and ask permission of no one where to go or how long to stay. Lt Col Pride writing in the Liverpool Courier on 11th October 1900 was more concerned about the conifers and over thinning for he preferred the birch and the sycamore.

Difficulties were experienced with Corsican pine establishment and a report of 29th September 1902 stated that losses were particularly heavy that year due to severe weather after planting [33]. Partly as a result of this it was decided to raise seedlings in the Delamere nursery instead of buying in, and in April 1903 one kilo of Scots pine seed and one kilo of Corsican pine seed was ordered from Conrad Appel, a seed merchant in Darmstadt, Germany at a cost including postage of 13s 3d [34]. However they still needed to buy in some plants and for instance Scots pine was obtained from Clibran of Hale and Corsican pine from Dicksons of Chester in 1905. Further seed including Weymouth pine was ordered from Conrad Appel in 1906 by the then forester Mr A Saunders.

Forestry Consultant E P Popert draws up a Working Plan, 1908

In 1908, the Commissioner of Woods, Earl Carrington, appointed a Consultant forester, E P Popert of Braceland, Coleford, Gloucestershire and instructed him to draw up a new working plan. In November that year Popert submitted his working plan to the Commissioner [35]. Except for the 541 acres which had been planted since 1893 and 55 acres which were being regenerated naturally with Scots pine, Popert planned to clear and replant for no part of the remainder was worth retaining.

Conifers would be planted on 918 acres. The main species would be Scots pine with a large proportion of Corsican pine, except on the moist ground where spruce would be planted and Sitka spruce tried.

Broadleaved trees would be planted on 284 acres of sandy loam, where oak would be the principal species using three year old stock planted at four feet espacement. When it reached the pole stage it would be underplanted with beech. Belts of deciduous trees would be retained along the roads as a fire precaution measure.

Replanting would be at the approximate rate of 40 acres of conifer and 20 acres of hardwood a year, and the whole 1,202 acres would be completed in 22 years.

Gaps in the conifer replanting caused by deaths from honey fungus, would be filled with chestnut and false acacia. Account was taken of possible insect attacks on the pine. Replanting would be arranged in five series of coupes so that extensive cleared blocks would not occur. This would help to check explosions in the insect population, provide shelter from the wind, and reduce drying out of the soil.

Popert used the compartmentation and numbers that Spencer Gore had drawn up in 1893 and described the condition of each of the fifty compartments and treatment proposed in a systematic and succinct way.

He assumed the conifers would be grown on a 60 year rotation when 3,000 cubic feet of timber would be obtained, while the oak would be run on a 120 year rotation when a final yield of 4,000 cubic feet would result. He confidently forecast that there would be no difficulty in disposing of all the timber profitably, as the forest is conveniently situated for export and near to large towns.

In 1908, the workforce consisted of a resident woodman and four permanent labourers. He recommended that four more permanent labourers should be employed, for casual labour even if it could be procured is not satisfactory.

By 1912, the young plantations had increased to 770 acres, and Sitka spruce was being tried in the damp parts. Certainly some of the plantation establishment was being very successfully achieved for Mr Saunders, the Forester, collected first and second prizes at the 1910 Royal Agricultural Society Show at Liverpool for two plantations at Delamere [36].

There were also problems, particularly with insect pests. Forester Saunders reported extensive infestation of pine by the sawfly, *Lophyrus rufus*, in June 1912, and attacks by the pine shoot tortrix, *Rhyacionia buoliana*, on 6 to 16 year old trees [37]. Later in Volume 6 of the *Journal of Forestry* he described the sawfly attack as a severe one over 500 to 600 acres of plantation. Both Scots, Corsican, and Weymouth pines were defoliated. Control work was carried out by men going in line through the plantations crushing the caterpillars in their hands. In 1916, there was a severe attack of pine weevil, *Hylobius abieti*, in a newly planted crop. The weevils were picked off by hand by women and then burnt [38].

Because there was little timber of value in the forest and young crops had not yet come into production, there was no pressure to cut timber in Delamere in the first World War despite the national shortage. There was considerable concern nationally about available wood supplies during the 1914 - 18 war, when it became apparent that timber was essential for economic survival. As a result of this the Forestry Sub Committee was set up in 1916 under the chairmanship of the Rt Hon F D Acland MP, to consider and report upon the best means of conserving and developing the woodland and forest resources of the United Kingdom, having regard to the experience gained during the war.

The subsequent report published in May 1917 became known as the Acland Report. Its proposals for forest policy and the establishment of a forest authority were accepted and the Forestry Act 1919 provided the necessary legislation for the Forestry Commission to be set up under the chairmanship of Lord Lovat [39].

Subsequently, in 1923, the Forestry (Transfer of Woods) Act enabled control of Delamere forest to be transferred from the Commissioner of Woods to the Forestry Commission.

The Forestry Commission at Delamere

The new era commenced in 1924 when the 1,839 acres in the forest were transferred to the Forestry Commission. There was much work to be done for no thinnings had been carried out in the crops replanted from 1893 on, and only part of Popert's replanting programme had been accomplished. The work started by Spencer Gore in 1893, continued and expanded into a long term working plan by Popert in 1908, laid the base on which the Forestry Commission developed the forest we know today.

The thinning programme was given high priority for trees were very closely spaced with whippy small crowns. Most of the early planting had been carried out at a four foot espacement and sometimes three. Even so it was 1928 before thinning really got going and because of the close spacing of the trees it had to be done in stages over several years to avoid excessive wind blow.

Stem diameters were very small but, despite the large quantity of material harvested, markets were found for it as rustic poles, packing rods for nurserymen for use in fruit tree despatch, flower and tomato stakes, and a host of other uses. Birch brush cleaned out of young pine plantations in Delamere was sold to racecourses for making steeplechase jumps, including those on the Grand National course at Aintree[40].

From 1924, plants used in the replanting programme were almost all produced in nurseries within the forest. Because of the scarcity of oak mast only six acres of the oak prescribed for planting by Popert on the better soils had been planted by 1930 [41].

One of the silvicultural operations introduced was that of high pruning selected pines to a height of 30 feet, which cost 3d - 3½d per tree in 1934-8. The object of this was to produce a higher quality and cleaner log and achieve an enhanced price for final crop trees [42].

Though few provisions were made for public use in the interwar years, it was a popular place for nearby townsfolk to visit and enjoy a day out in the quiet of the forest. There was always some concern in the periods of fire hazard, the greatest risk normally being from February to May when there is much dead and dry vegetation remaining from winter before new growth appears. Fire fighters were called out by a bugle call from Pale Heights [43].

There were considerable wartime fellings in the forest. Between 1940 and 1945, 342 acres were clearfelled, 1,092 acres received a second thinning, and 366 acres were thinned for the first time, yielding almost one million hoppus feet of produce. The felling was mainly carried out by the Timber Production Department which was set up during the war to meet the national need for timber [44]. Some of the best old stands were saved from felling. Most of the produce went as pitprops for the mines and some went for woodwool production for use mainly in ropes and packaging.

Delamere was always noted for its forest insects and was a mecca for forest entomologists and students. Among the many forest pests were the pine weevil, *Hylobius abietis*, the black pine beetle, *Hylastes ater*, the pine sawfly, *Diprion pini*, the pine shoot moth, *Evetria buoliana*, the large pine shoot beetle, *Tomicus abietina*, and the spruce aphid, *Neomyzaphis abietina*. There were particularly high populations in 1900-30 due largely to overdue thinning and general neglect, and again in the second war years due to stacked unpeeled material lying in the forest for considerable periods awaiting transport. The latter provided ideal breeding grounds for the pine shoot beetle and pine weevil [45].

Late frosts frequently occur at Delamere, and they are particularly damaging to spruce. This is one reason why Popert's plan to grow Sitka spruce on moist sites proved unsuccessful. Even if it got through the frosts this tree would have been unlikely to flourish in later years, on account of the comparatively low rainfall of approximately 800mm per year.

Corsican pine is now the main tree planted in Delamere, for it has proved the most productive species for the conditions, though Scots pine is also used. The forest is now essentially a pine forest with small areas of hardwood particularly along the roadsides. The wide range of age classes in the pine varying from a few old stands dating back to the end of the 19th century, some of which still contain a few Weymouth pine, to newly planted areas, make it a most attractive forest much used by the public.

The public came by train and by car to the forest in large numbers even though there were no particular facilities provided for them, and there was widespread congestion at bank holidays and weekends. In 1969 to celebrate their first fifty years the Forestry Commission opened a small visitor centre and established some guided trails in the forest, while provision for parking was made along the switchback and station roads.

The forest itself is now approximately 800 hectares in extent, consisting of a main block and eight smaller outliers. Approximately 6,000 cubic metres of softwood timber are produced every year, the bulk coming from the annual cut of mature woodland, and the remainder from young plantations which are thinned every five years.

Because of the diversity of age classes and sensitive replanting and management, which now balances forestry and environmental needs, there is a wide range of habitat and wealth of wild life to be found in Delamere.

Delamere attained the status of a Forest Park in 1987 and public provisions include an enlarged visitor centre with shop and educational facilities. The County Council provide a Countryside Ranger service both to assist the public and to help with the maintenance of the trails, parking and picnic sites, and other public provision.

The policy is to provide visitors with the opportunity to follow a wide range of quiet countryside pursuits in a forest setting, with minimum detriment to wildlife and the ecology and working of the forest. Over 250,000 people visit the forest every year. All these activities have been fitted into a timber producing commercial forest. Felling, replanting, thinning, and other forest operations are carried out as is normal in a managed forest producing industrial timber, operations which are there for the public to see. At any one time only a small part of the forest is affected so there are always large areas where the peace and quiet of the forest can be enjoyed.

Macclesfield Forest

Little remains of the Royal Forest except for a few scattered remnants of ancient woodland in private ownership, and some boundary stones. Most of the land was enclosed and devoted to farming, with sheep predominating in the upland areas.

The population of Macclesfield increased rapidly during the Industrial Revolution, while many new mills were built as the silk industry developed in the 19th century. To meet the demand for water Ridgegate Reservoir was constructed in 1850 at Langley, together with Bottoms and Teggs Nose Reservoirs, and Trentabank Reservoir was constructed in 1929. Macclesfield Corporation purchased farms in the Trentabank and Ridgegate catchment area and decided that the land was most suitable for growing timber, as it would conserve the catchment, provide clean water, and produce a return.

Afforestation of the farmland, which was situated on the lower slopes of the Pennines above the reservoirs just to the east of Macclesfield, commenced in 1931. The forest now covers an area of almost 400 hectares, with its highest point 480 metres. The main tree species grown are Japanese larch and Sitka spruce, the latter being much more at home here with a rainfall of 1000mm and few late frost problems. Other species planted include the Scots, Corsican and Lodgepole pines, Norway spruce, beech, and sycamore.

The forest is now owned by the Northwest Water Company, who manage it on a commercial basis with an annual production programme in the long term plan. In addition to thinning, some felling is being carried out to create a wider range of age classes. In replanting the opportunity is being taken to introduce more broadleaves into the forest where soils are suitable, and to bring more diversity to the forest landscape.

The plantations provide a fine setting to the reservoirs and contribute much to the attractive scene. There is a network of well marked footpaths through the forest and a carpark is provided at the centre close to Trentabank Reservoir. The stonewalls that marked the old field boundaries are still on the ground though often hidden in the trees.

There is a varied wildlife population enhanced by waterfowl on the reservoirs. The activity in the heronry among some larch trees on a promontory on Trentabank Reservoir can be clearly seen from the nearby road, particularly in early spring before the leaf is on the larch when the herons are rebuilding their nests and flying in with sticks from the forest. An itinerant herd of red deer frequently uses the forest and can occasionally be seen.

CHAPTER 10 - The Victorian Parks

The Shrewsbury MP Robert Slaney was one of the main spokesmen in the House of Commons in 1833 when he argued the case for improving the living conditions of the working classes in cities and towns where areas were needed for healthful exercise and air. His proposal to form a Select Committee to carry out 'An enquiry into the means of providing open spaces in the vicinity of populous towns as public walks and places of exercise, calculated to promote the health and happiness and comfort of the inhabitants' was adopted and Robert Slaney was appointed its Chairman. The movement towards the provision of public open space gained momentum but it was almost impossible for local authorities to buy land for this purpose except by Act of Parliament until the 1848 Public Health Act enabled municipal authorities to purchase and maintain land for parks [1].

There had been a period of immense growth particularly in the manufacturing towns where workers were housed in row upon row of terraces, usually living in overcrowded conditions with no garden, while there was rarely any open space around the factories and mills in which they worked.

A special Act of Parliament was passed in 1843 to allow Birkenhead to proceed with an innovative scheme to buy land and create a public park. With a government loan of £60,000, borrowed on behalf of the ratepayers, Birkenhead acquired 226 acres and used 125 of them to provide a public open space in perpetuity for the free recreation of the town's inhabitants, and sold off the remaining 101 acres as building plots. It became known as the People's Park [2].

The park was designed by Joseph Paxton and gained a reputation as one of the great designer's masterpieces. Edward Kemp, who had trained under Paxton at Chatsworth, came to Birkenhead in 1843 to supervise the construction of the park. He must have impressed the authorities with his skill for he was appointed Park Superintendent in 1845. Alas, many of the trees Edward Kemp planted are no longer there, for the elms were ravaged by disease and trees have been lost through old age and other causes. Some new planting has taken place in recent years.

Kemp was allowed to take on outside commissions, and as the Birkenhead News described in his obituary in March 1891, he was constantly engaged over the length and breadth of the land. In 1857 his status was such that New York Park Commission consulted him concerning their proposed competition for a design for Central Park, New York.

Certainly his reputation had reached the ear of the Marquess of Westminster in 1866, for he engaged him to design and supervise the landscaping in his new park by the River Dee in Chester. John Douglas was engaged as the architect. The new park was presented to the city the following year when planting was complete. It is now known as Grosvenor Park and being so close to the centre of Chester, adjoining the ancient church of St Johns and overlooking the river, it is extensively used by the public.

The planting plan showing the position and species of trees and shrubs planted can be seen at Chester City Record Office. The plants were supplied by Francis and Arthur Dickson & Sons from their Upton nurseries. The order included 200 large selected lime at 6d each and 136 specimen Pyramidal Hodgins holly at 10/- each, the most expensive tree used. Most of the lime and the Pyramidal holly were used as alternate trees in the magnificent avenues, such a notable feature of the park planted in 1866 and flourishing today. A good proportion of the trees originally planted are still to be found though every one of the 356 elms used has been lost through disease. There has been an active replacement programme and a wide range of species is represented in this well maintained park.

The purchase of land for West Park Macclesfield, which was opened in 1854, was funded by public subscription inaugurated in 1851. It was created to commemorate the Repeal of the Corn Laws and the workers of Macclesfield contributed £300 of the £1,850 purchase price, the balance and the cost of construction being met by subscriptions from local gentry [3]. Aptly it was created on the site of the original Macclesfield Townfield, where the Macclesfield Races had been held. One of the objectives was to provide a place for athletic amusement. Mr William Barron, a Scotsman from Berwick, who was the Earl of Harrington's nurseryman and landscape gardener at Elvaston and visited Gawsworth regularly, had much to do with the design and planting of the park. Barron had worked with Joseph Paxton at Sydenham Palace, London.

The Park covers an area of 16 acres. Adjoining it to the north on the other side of the Whitfield Brook, is the Macclesfield Cemetery, which was consecrated in 1866. On the slope above the brook is a small but notable pinetum probably established just after this date. In the Macclesfield Courier and Herald report on the consecration dated 19th May 1866 it states that 'The grounds are being beautifully laid out with gravel walks and flower beds, the planting having been arranged and executed by Mr Middlebrook, the Curator of the Public Park'.

A small arboretum has recently been established within the park on the bank on the south side of the Whitfield Brook. It includes 22 species chosen by the Lady Mayoress, Councillor Sue Hardern and the Environmental Committee in 1990. Particularly appropriate to the town of Macclesfield is the choice of a white mulberry, the species preferred by silkworms. The selection of both a dawn redwood and a swamp cypress will enable these two deciduous conifers, very similar in appearance, to be compared in close proximity.

Victoria Park, Macclesfield was presented to the town in 1894 by Mr Francis D Brocklehurst. 13 acres of land including Fence House were donated. The house was dismantled but many of the mature trees surrounding it were retained, including fine lime, horse chestnut and beech together with the original thorn walk.

The inscription on the monument in the park reads 'Erected by the inhabitants of Macclesfield to record the name of Charles Brocklehurst Esq of The Fence, and to perpetuate the memory of his untiring labours for the welfare of his fellow townsmen'. This is an attractive small park with fine mature trees bordering Fence Road, but the range of species is limited.

Queens Park, Crewe was opened by HRH The Duke of Cambridge in June 1888. This fine park covering 45 acres was presented to the town by the London North Western Railway at a dedication ceremony in 1887 when the company's chairman Sir Richard Moon Bt was made the first honorary freeman of the borough. 1887 was the year of Queen Victoria's Jubilee and it was also fifty years since the Great Junction Railway had been opened. The oval shaped park had been designed and laid out by Edward Kemp and F W Webb on fields adjoining the old sewerage works, a small part of which was included in the park area. Use was made of the Valley Brook and natural features to construct a lake in the southern part of the park. The lake with its islands is a delightful feature, enhanced by groups of specimen trees on the grass slopes running down to its edge.

Just below the cafeteria a Judas tree, *Cercis siliquastrum*, can be found, most evident in late May or early June when it is covered in rose pink blossom. The flowers of this small tree are unusual for they arise directly from the bark. The leaves are shaped rather like an ear. The species was introduced to this country in the 16th century from the eastern Mediterranean, where it is reputed to be the tree on which Judas hanged himself. There is a wide tree lined avenue leading down from the lodges to the war memorial of unusual design. Either side of the drive is a widely spaced line of silver birch with a similar line of sycamore on the outside, and low growing yew between the two lines. The design is spacious and the contrast in colour, texture, and form between sycamore and birch is striking. A wide selection of tree species including many conifers can be found within the park, which is a particularly fine one and an asset to the town.

The guiding hand of Joseph Paxton or Edward Kemp has been a major factor in fashioning the planted Victorian landscape in Cheshire, both in public parks and in the gardens surrounding Victorian mansions, for Kemp particularly, undertook a large number of private commissions in the Birkenhead and Chester areas. Many of the trees they planted are becoming overmature, particularly if they are conifers, and their replacement is a challenging task which must be addressed if these invaluable landscape features are to be perpetuated.

17. Queen's Park, Crewe at the time of its opening, June 1888. Illustrated London News Picture Library.

CHAPTER 11 - Arboreta and Tree Collections

The principal arboreta and tree collections in the county are listed alphabetically. There are also many smaller collections of specimen trees on the landed estates and elsewhere which contribute so much to the rich variety of species in the landscape.

Arley Hall - The Grove [OS SJ 677810]

This is a large collection of mainly ornamental trees dispersed through an area of open woodland and garden just to the northeast of the Hall. It was started in a small way by the Hon Michael Flower over twenty years ago, but it has gradually been extended by adding species each year. The *Acers* are well represented with over 20 species or varieties, which with *Nyssa sylvatica, Liquidambar, Parrotia* and many species of *Sorbus* and *Prunus* adding to the colour, makes it well worth an autumn visit. It is also a collection to see in the spring when the numerous varieties of *Magnolia* are in flower as well as *Prunus, Malus* and other spring flowering trees. It is open with Arley Gardens from 12 noon to 5pm Tuesday to Sunday every week from the end of March to the beginning of October, and Bank Holiday Mondays within this period.

Cholmondeley Castle Gardens [OS SJ 537514]

The gardens on the slopes below the castle date back to the beginning of the 19th century when Cholmondeley Castle was built, and the large cedars of Lebanon and other mature trees probably date back to that time. Many new trees and shrubs were planted in the 1950s and later, and there is now a fine collection of trees to be found dispersed through the garden area in most attractive surroundings.

The collection includes the unusual variegated form of the tulip tree, *Liriodendron tulipifera 'Auromarginatum'*, one of the more uncommon silver firs, *Abies delavayi georgei*, with its purplish cones and upright pointed bracts, and the cow's tail pine, *Cephalotaxus harringtonia*, a bushy member of the yew family with leaves in two ranks curving upwards from the shoot looking rather like the wings of a dove, and many other interesting species.

The gardens are open on Sundays and Bank Holidays from Easter to mid October 12 noon to 5.30pm.

Coomb Dale Pinetum [OS SJ 510541]

This private collection was started by Mr A G Barbour about twenty years ago in a sheltered fold in the Bickerton Hills. The light sandstone derived and slightly acid soils are well suited to most conifers. The 60 species represented include 15 different pines, 15 species of silver fir, and 11 different spruces, growing on the bracken covered slopes in scenic surroundings.

Foxhill Arboretum [OS SJ 508753]

Dr L H A Pilkington started this extensive private collection in 1967 on the wooded slopes of Frodsham Hill. Existing overmature beech and pine has gradually been cleared to make space for planting a wide range of species on the slightly acid light soils over the sandstone. The oaks are particularly well represented for 20 different species have been planted. They are still quite small so it is the conifers which are most noticeable at present. These include 10 species of silver fir and representatives of most families.

Jodrell Bank, The Granada Arboretum [OS SJ 798712]

Work on this arboretum was commenced in 1972 with initial funding from the Northern Arts and Sciences Foundation and land provided by the University of Manchester. The idea was hatched a year earlier by Sir Bernard Lovell, founder and first director of the Nuffield Radio Astronomy Laboratories at Jodrell Bank, and Sir William Mather a leading industrialist who is also closely connected with the Granada Foundation, after an approach by Professor Graham Ashworth then director of the Civic Trust. Professor D H Valentine and Dr R A Benton of the University of Manchester Botany Department helped to draw up the plans and the first trees were planted late in 1972.

The arboretum was created on 35 acres of exposed meadowland . Most of the first planting was carried out with birch, Scots pine and larch to provide the shelter within which collections of family groups of trees could be introduced. It now holds nationally designated collections of *Sorbus* and *Malus* among over 2,500 species, varieties, and cultivars of trees and shrubs which are continually being added to. There is a particularly large collection of varieties of the Lawsons cypress together with trees grown from seed from natural stands of the species in Oregon.

Although only twenty years old the arboretum is already a most attractive feature with plenty to interest knowledgeable tree lovers and those wanting to find out more about trees. As each year goes by it will become even more interesting as specimens mature, and for instance the fine young Antarctic beech, *Nothofagus antarctica*, now about 7 metres high could be more than double the size by the turn of the century.

The arboretum is open from 10.30am to 5.30pm daily from Easter to October, and from 12 noon to 5pm at weekends only for the remainder of the year. Group visits and school parties can be arranged throughout the year. An environmental visitor centre which provides information on trees and forestry was opened in spring 1992.

Linmere Arboretum, Delamere Forest [OS SJ 546704]

The Forestry Commission started to establish a small arboretum at Linmere a few years ago. Among the stock that it is intended to grow are most of the different species grown in the state forests together with those used in motorway planting. The trees are still very young so defer a visit for a few years unless you are in the area.

Ness Gardens [OS SJ 305755]

These gardens were started in 1898 by A K Bulley who acquired the property as a site for raising seed for commercial purposes and receiving material from plant collectors he had commissioned, such as George Forrest and Frank Kingdon Ward. Material came from all over the world, but particularly the Far East. Plants were grown on in the gardens to test both their suitability for British conditions and the commercial market. This was the start of Bees Ltd, the nursery company which Mr Bulley later moved to a large 1,000 acre site at Sealand, Chester.

Ness lies close to sea level by the estuary of the Dee and it is very exposed to westerly gales. Shelterbelts of evergreen oak, Scots, Corsican and Austrian pines, and poplar were planted early this century, and within these the gardens were established. Miss A L Bulley gave the 35 acre estate to Liverpool University in 1948. It has since been enlarged to 50 acres and developed as the University Botanic Gardens.

There are many specimen trees and shrubs including a fine Pin oak, *Quercus*

18. The Duke of Windsor planting a Deodar Cedar at Reaseheath in 1926. Reaseheath College Archives.

palustris, several dove trees, *Davidia involucrata*, and an extensive collection of *Sorbus* including the species *Forrestii*, the Chinese rowan. The latter was identified by Deputy Director Dr Hugh McAllister in 1980 though it was collected by Forrest in Western China in 1921. These are but a few of the many species to be found in the gardens.

Ness keeps a national willow collection which is the duplicate of the one maintained at Long Ashton Research Station. Clones were transferred between 1983 and 1985 when the Research Station was threatened with closure. Currently extensive trials are being carried out on a wide range of species of birch, alder, and whitebeam.

The Friends of Ness Gardens arrange lectures and demonstrations of horticultural techniques outthe year and publish a quarterly newsletter. The gardens are open daily from 9.30am to 4pm November to February, and 9.30am to dusk for the remainder of the year.

Reaseheath College Arboretum and Gardens [OS SJ 647541]

Work on the aboretum has started recently with small collections of ash and oak species planted in groups on the edge of the golf course. Far more interesting at this stage is the collection of mature trees in the gardens. Among the cedars which are well represented pride of place must go to the very fine specimen of *Cedrus brevifolia* with its multi stems and well-shaped crown which is growing by the lakeside. There are well-grown mature Atlantic and Deodar cedars to be found, together with a younger Deodar which was planted by the Duke of Windsor in 1926. Another outstanding tree is the fern leaved beech, an attractive cultivar of the common beech with narrow cut leaves, which is among the best in the county. These are but a few of the many species to be found in these well maintained woodland gardens.

The college holds open days during the year when the gardens can be visited.

Swettenham, The Quinta Arboretum [OS SJ 799671]

This privately owned arboretum was started by Sir Bernard Lovell when he acquired some exposed agricultural land adjoining his garden. It is now some 17 acres in extent and contains a wide range of trees and shrubs from most parts of the world which he had seen and sometimes collected on his many visits to scientific institutions overseas.

The layout is most attractive, divided up by grass rides and some impressive avenues. One of red twigged lime, *Tilia platyphyllos rubra*, is known as the Reith Avenue for it was planted in 1957-8 at the time Sir Bernard delivered the Reith Lectures. It is already some 15 metres in height.

Species of pine, birch, oak, apple, and whitebeam are well represented, while there are a wealth of others including four species of the winged nut, *Pterocarya*, and some rarities. The latter include the gutta-percha tree, *Eucommia ulmoides*, the sassafras, *Sassifras albidum*, and the extraordinary *Laburnocytisus adamii*, a graft hybrid of laburnum and purple broom which originated in a Paris nursery. Some branches bear the flowers of purple broom and other flowers of yellow laburnum.

The arboretum and gardens have been open to the public in past years under the National Gardens Scheme on particular days, and it is intended to open them again in the future.

Tatton Park, Pinetum and Gardens [OS SJ 743814]

The pinetum situated in the southwest corner of the gardens, contains trees collected by the Egerton family since the end of the 19th century. This is a particularly fine collection of conifers including some of considerable age. Of the many spruces represented which include the red spruce, oriental spruce, and Engelmann's spruce, there is a fine specimen of the Morinda or West Himalayan spruce, *Picea smithiana*, approximately 25 metres high and 2.2 metres in girth at 1.5 metres above ground level. Outside the pinetum close to Lady Charlotte's arbour stands an excellent young Brewer spruce, *Picea breweriana*, about 9 metres high which is surely one of the most beautiful of evergreen weeping trees.

Many species of pine, cypress, hemlock, and silver fir can be found in the pinetum. Just outside it by the Japanese garden, which is one of the finest in the

19. The Pleasure Gardens at Tatton Park, 1890.
Illustrated London News Picture Library

country, is a well-furnished specimen of the Japanese umbrella pine, *Sciadopytis verticillata*, with its unusual whorls of shiny green, long, needle-like grooved leaves which are evenly spaced along the shoots. There is a group of dawn redwood, *Metasequoia glyptostroboides*, to be found close to the Tower Garden, a tree first found growing in southwest China in 1941 and previously known only as a fossil.

There is a wealth of interest for the tree lover at Tatton and some of the trees are labelled to help identification. The gardens, including the pinetum, are open daily except for Monday from 10.30am.

20. Rustic Bridge in the gardens at Tatton Park, 1890.
Illustrated London News Picture Library.

CHAPTER 12 - Historic and Notable Trees

Cheshire is extraordinarily rich in its heritage of fine mature landscape trees, thanks to the foresight of our ancestors who planted and maintained them. Though none appears in the list of Champion Trees of the British Isles which is based on maximum size, there is a great quality and diversity to be found in the range of species represented in the county, while some of our trees are of considerable antiquity and curiosity.

Trees have always been planted to celebrate events and long may that tradition continue. Single trees, avenues, groups, sometimes woods have been planted to mark coronations, jubilees, births, deaths, victories such as Trafalgar and Quebec, and in one case at Eaton, General Egerton is said to have laid out a mock battle of Agincourt [1].

One of the woodland curiosities is Maggoty Johnson's Wood at Gawsworth, OS SJ888702, a small mature mixed woodland in which Samuel Johnson, dancing master to Lord Harrington's children, was buried in 1773. He has been described as the last English jester and his ultimate joke was to be buried in the quiet of this wood rather than in the churchyard at Gawsworth. The inscription over his grave describes his life and wishes:-

> Under this stone rest the remains of Mr Samuel Johnson, afterwards enobled with the grander title of Lord Flame, who, after having been in his life distinct from other men, by the eccentricities of his genius, chose to retain the same character after his death. And was on his own desire buried here May 5th AD MDCCLXIII, aged 82. Stay thou whom chance directs or ease persuades to seek the quiet of these silvan shades. Here undisturbed hid from vulgar eyes, a wit, musician, poet, player lies. A dancing master to in grace he shone, and all the arts of opera were his own. In comedy well skilled, he drew Lord Flame, acted the part and gained himself the name. Averse to strife how oft he'd gravely say, these peaceful groves should shade his breathless day. That when he rose again laid here alone, no friend and he should quarrel for a bone. Thinking that some lame gossip nigh, she possibly might take his leg or thigh.

Maggoty Johnson's Wood is managed by the National Trust and is open to the public at all times.

The notable trees that are described are just some of those to be found around the county. Readers are invited to write to the Cheshire Landscape Trust giving details of others or to let their Parish Tree Warden know about them.

21. Lord Flame's grave in Maggoty Johnson's Wood, Gawsworth.

The Appleton Thorn

It is reputed that the first Appleton Thorn was planted about 1178 when Adam de Dutton, a Norman knight, returned from the crusades bringing a shoot of the Glastonbury Thorn with him.

The thorn is shown on a 1760 map of Sir Peter Warburton's lands in Appleton on the northwest side of the crossroads, but it would not have been the original tree for thorns do not have long lives. The latest replacement was in 1991 when a young Glastonbury Thorn, *Crataegus monogyna 'Biflora'* was specially obtained and planted following the loss of the previous tree in a gale.

At the crossroads the tree was in an important position and may well have been used as a meeting point in the early days. When the ceremony of Bawming The Thorn first arose is not known, but it is an ancient custom observed on or near 15th July, old mid summer's day. Bawming is the dialect word for adorning or anointing. In the ceremony the branches of the tree are decorated with red ribbons, posies, flower garlands, and flags. Villagers dance around the tree singing the Bawming Song to the tune of Bonnie Dundee with chorus words:-

Up with the fresh garlands this mid-summer morn
Up with red ribbons on Appleton Thorn
Come lasses and lads to the thorn tree today
To bawm it, and shout as ye bawm it Hurray.

The words were written by R E Egerton-Warburton of Arley in around 1870, but it may have replaced an earlier song[2]. The custom lapsed from time to time this century, but it was revived in 1973.

The Glastonbury Thorn produces both flowers and young foliage in winter as well as flowering at the normal time, so the belief that it breaks into flower on Christmas Day has some basis in fact in Glastonbury, for if the early part of the winter is mild it could have blossom in January. Old Christmas Day was on 6th January. Here at Appleton Thorn, being that much further north, the tree is unlikely to produce flowers so early.

The Beech (*Fagus sylvatica*)

Beech grows particularly well in east Cheshire often attaining great size. Some of the oldest are at Dunham Massey dating back to 1714 at Langham Grove, and at Tatton Park where a few of the beech planted along with Scots pine in the avenue to Knutsford around 1720, still remain, the largest having a diameter of 151cm at 1.5m. None of the earliest beech planting by the mere at Alderley in 1650 remains, but there is a very old and large tree on the edge of Boys Walk which is approximately 31m high with a magnificent butt 165cm in diameter at 1.5m. The mature beech on Alderley Edge were planted in 1799.

Good examples of the fern-leaved beech, *Fagus sylvatica heterophylla*, can be seen at Reaseheath College and at Marbury Country Park where there is a specimen close by the Fastigiate oak, but the largest located to date is growing at Foxhill. This tree has a diameter at 1.5m of 103cm and a height of 22m. The cut leaves and rounded spreaded crown make this a most ornamental tree.

The weeping beech, *Fagus sylvatica pendula*, is another attractive variety and there is a magnificent specimen in the Rectory garden at Mobberley which has a spread of 20m, height of 9.8m and diameter at 1.5m of 60cm. The Rector passes through this weeping mobile wall of myriads of beech branches every time he goes to and from St Wilfred's Church. Under the tree itself it is like being in a green marquee.

No mature fastigiate Dawyck beech, *Fagus sylvatica fastigiata*, are known but there are two good semi-mature trees on the green outside St John's Church, Chester, showing the typical columnar habit, and there must be others. The tree gets its name from the Dawyck Estate near Peebles, where the variety originated. There are also many superb mature copper beeches to be found throughout the county, including a notable avenue along Manchester Road, Wilmslow where the occasional intermittent whitebeam and birch serve to emphasise the deep copper colour.

The Black Poplar (*Populus nigra var. betulifolia*)

This tree is native to Cheshire which is close to the northern limit of its range. It grows into a very large tree, characterised by a heavy rounded crown and irregular branching with the lower branches often arching to the ground. Normally propagated from cuttings, it is the male tree that has been planted most often for it has attractive red catkins. Also as poplars frequently hybridise it is not easy to find the true native tree, while it is very rare to find both sexes growing together [3]. Such a situation exists at Foxes Farm, Ledsham on the farm boundary by a marl pit, where two female and one male poplar are growing in close proximity to each other.

There is a good example of a mature female tree on the edge of the lane by Sealand Church, OS SJ353689. In the past these poplars have often been planted along lanes, footpaths, and boundaries, and were probably the poplar most often planted as a condition of farm leases in the 18th and 19th centuries. They are to be found throughout the county and grow into very large trees. The rounded heavily branched dense crowns of the native black poplar are a complete contrast to the tall, slender crowned, fastigiate black Italian poplars, *Populus nigra italica*, which have been described as exclamation marks in the landscape. The largest black poplar recorded to date, though not the true native variety, is standing in a hedgerow by a footpath at the Butts, Nether Alderley OS SJ 845770. This is a magnificent tree 33.5m (110') high with a diameter of 144cm at 1.5m.

False Acacia (*Robinia pseudoacacia*)

At the rear of Dunham Massey Hall on a mound by the lake which used to be the viewing point for the formal gardens stands a grove of mature *Robinia* with its typical deeply furrowed bark. Attractive creamy-white flowers are borne in June, but beware of the sharp and spiny stipules on the twigs.

A massive twin-stemmed specimen can be found at Delamere by the side of the track which leads past the visitor centre, OS SJ 548703. The tree is 19.8m high with stems of 81cm and 90cm diameter at 1.5m, and a basal circumference of 4.9m. *Robinia* makes an attractive street tree as can be seen in Saughall Road, Blacon, Chester and other urban locations.

Hornbeam (*Carpinus betulus*)

There is a magnificent specimen of this tree, with a deeply fluted clear bole of 10m looking like a mass of grey organ pipes, growing in the Wilderness at Adlington Estate, OS SJ 905801. This tree which is 90cm in diameter at 1.5m may not be the largest in the county but the fluting on the bole is quite exceptional. Its height is 21m.

The Limes

The native small-leaved lime, *Tilia cordata*, is rarely found, but Cheshire is particularly rich in notable avenues of the common lime, which is the much planted hybrid between *Tilia cordata* and *Tilia platyphillos*, the large-leaved lime.

The oldest avenue, said to have been planted in 1688 to celebrate the accession of William and Mary, leads to the old formal gardens and Wilderness at Adlington, OS SJ 905803. The average diameter at 1.5m is 126cm, on the small side for trees of this age, but all 18 trees were cut back in the past at a height of 2.5m, while they are closely spaced being 5.5m apart, so their growth may have been restricted.

There is a lovely grove of lime at Gawsworth just south of the old hall, containing both very old trees and ones recently planted, an ideal area for strolling and meditating. This is shown as planted on Grey's 1770 Estate Map so the oldest trees certainly predate this. The avenue along the road leading to the Harrington Arms is more recent, being planted in 1827 [4]. There is a small closely planted avenue of fine mature lime leading from the church at Malpas towards the Rectory, standing just 12 feet apart. This probably dates back to the mid 18th century. These are but a few examples of the many mature lime avenues to be found in the county.

Pleached lime avenues can be found at Arley Hall, planted in 1851, and at Parkside Hospital, Macclesfield. The Arley avenue is a particularly good example. Branches are trained horizontally so that the trees form a narrow screen maintained annually by clipping. This eventually produces a collonade effect which is clearly seen at Arley, where the pleached lime screen leads to the clock tower entrance. The Parkside Hospital example is more recent and the pleaching is raised higher up the boles.

One of the largest silver limes in Cheshire is situated in a private garden off Parkgate Road, Neston. Fortunately this specimen of *Tilia petiolaris* is well cared for as it grows in the garden of Mr J K Hulme, formerly director of Ness Gardens.

The Magnolia

A fine wide-crowned specimen of Campbell's magnolia, *Magnolia campbellii*, stands in a private garden at the corner of Wood Lane and Earls Drive, Parkgate. In early spring the huge rose pink flowers are a striking sight and residents from that part of the Wirral make detours in order to drive past and admire the display.

The Mulberry (*Morus species*)

The white mulberry, *Morus alba*, has the reputation of being the most favoured food plant of the Silk Moth, and in 1608 James I sent a circular letter to persons of influence in the country suggesting they might plant mulberries to encourage the silk industry. Arrangements were made for plant distribution and presumably some came to Cheshire estates at the time.

22. The magnificent fluted hornbeam at the Wilderness, Adlington.

23. The propped up mulberry at Knight's Grange, Winsford.

24. The ancient Marton Oak with the Wendy House within.

25. Lightning damaged the Marbury Oak planted in 1814 to commemorate Wellington's victory at Orthez.

Black mulberry, *Morus nigra*, was the most frequently planted. A typical spreading propped-up old specimen can be found in the garden of the Knight's Grange Inn, Winsford OS SJ 639671, and there are two good younger specimens outside the Barony Hospital, Nantwich OS SJ 654533, and there are others.

The Oaks, *Quercus* species

The county is renowned for its oaks for it is the predominant tree in the landscape, and there are magnificent examples of massive old trees to be found. There are past records too. In 1793 at Morley near Wilmslow a remarkable oak was felled, 41ft in circumference at the base and 32ft in circumference at a height of 12ft which had a huge cavity capable of admitting 6 - 8 people [5].

A tree at Dunham Massey which blew down in a gale in 1802, heronry and all, contained 403' of timber under bark of which 373½ hoppus feet were sold at 6s 6d per foot. Herons are very good at selecting the very finest oak timber trees for their nests as they have done at Combermere, but even the soundest of trees can blow in freak weather conditions. Some oak were not so large but perfectly shaped as the tree George Fox chose to preach under at Frandley by the road to Comberbach in 1660 on his way to London after imprisonment in Lancaster [6].

The largest remaining oak and probably the oldest, is the Marton Oak, situated in a private garden on the edge of the village of Marton OS SJ 853683, whose immense hollow bole once housed a calf shed and now encloses a Wendy house. Though but a shell of what must have been a monumental tree in its prime, there is plenty of life yet in this ancient relic of possibly 600 years, for the flattened 14m wide crown is well furnished with foliage. Now only 9.1m high, this tree has a girth of 13.4m (44') at 1.5m.

Almost as ancient must be the relic pollard oaks on an old field boundary close to Yew Tree Farm, Coddington OS SJ 464557, which can be seen from the road. Again these are hollow stumps of trees which have lived on and on with limited live branching, that even survived a stick of bombs which exploded a few metres away in the last war. The largest tree has a diameter of 189cm at 1.5m height.

One of the two fine mature oak trees depicted in a George Stubbs painting, Mares And Foals dated about 1766, still stands in a field close to the Eaton Estate Office. This is another hollow tree whose diameter is 167cm at 1.5m, which is estimated to be 450 years old. The other blew down some years ago. There are other larger oaks in the park and grounds of the Westminster Estate which must be older, though size is not always indicative of age.

There are also magnificent old parkland trees on the Combermere Estate of great age, including one in which the king is reputed to have hidden during the Civil War. The Cholmondeley Estate and Tatton Park also contain many fine oaks. At the latter OS SJ 751827, there is an old hollow tree known as the King Charles Oak, which received some early tree surgery - a rusty iron brace and chain holding one of the limbs.

In the 19th century Alderley Park and Dunham Massey were reputed to have the greatest stocks of oak timber, and the deer park at Dunham still contains many ancient trees with their crowns raised by persistent browsing by deer. Many trees are dying back at the top and contain much deadwood as well as decay in the bole, so it is one of the richest sites in the country for deadwood beetle fauna and was declared a site of Special Scientific Interest (SSSI) for that reason.

On Arley Green, OS SJ 682807, a large oak can be found with an iron bar closing off a hollow at the base of the massive stem. This was fitted a few years ago to remove the temptation for children to crawl into the tree and possibly get stuck in the process. Some years prior to that a former squire of Arley is said to have squeezed 11 boys inside the oak, paying the 1/- each for their discomfort[7].

On the roadside opposite the entrance to Peckforton Castle, OS SJ 538576, an oak 21.6m in height and 206cm in diameter at 1.5m, is a majestic tree with a very heavy crown. An older but hollow oak at Tushingham Hall, OS SJ 529450, has a much larger diameter of 243cm at 1.5m and you can sense the history in its ancient gnarled butt. The crown is a relic but the tree will probably live on for many more years.

The Marbury Oak by the inn, OS SJ 562458, was planted in 1814 to commemorate Wellington's victory over Soult at Orthez. It is now a well-shaped tree 118cm in diameter at 1.5m, but unfortunately it was damaged by lightning some years ago and the resulting scar can be clearly seen on the bole. General Combermere fought with the Duke of Wellington who planted an oak when he came to visit the Combermere Estate in a wood along the Shropshire border, now known as Wellington Wood.

The Bostock Oak was planted in what was considered to be the exact centre of Cheshire in 1887 to celebrate Queen Victoria's Jubilee. This tree can be found in a small enclosure at Bostock Green, OS SJ 672693, on the side of the A533. Commemorative plaques mark the event. It is a comparatively small tree with a height of 12.8m and a diameter of 66cm at 1.5m.

One of the largest and oldest specimens of evergreen oak, *Quercus ilex*, is situated close to the mere and abbey at Combermere, but there are trees on most estates. It is particularly frequent close to the coast in the Wirral. In the gardens at Arley Hall there is a unique avenue of clipped barrel-shaped trees which were planted some 130 years ago. They were badly frosted in the winter of 1981-2 and for some months the trees looked as if they might not recover, but miraculously the avenue returned to its former glory.

The Lucombe oak is a hybrid between the Cork oak and the Turkey oak, which normally keeps its dark green leaves into the spring. There is an excellent example

26. The Bostock Oak, planted in 1887 to mark the centre of Cheshire.

of this tree on the Henbury Estate in the park northwest of the hall, while there are many of these trees surrounding the Hoole Hall Hotel in Chester of a good age. Cork oak, *Quercus suber*, can be seen in Dunham Massey garden. The Turkey oak, *Quercus cerris*, is found in most of the parks, but there are particularly good specimens at Marbury Country Park, Northwich, OS SJ 651764, and unusually there is a small plantation of mature trees of this species at Fox Covert close to Tattenhall, OS SJ 498584. Also at Marbury Country Park there is a mature fastigiate oak, *Quercus robur fastigiata*, probably planted around 1850-60, 22m in height and 76cm in diameter at 1.5m. It is best viewed in winter when it is easier to see the upright branching habit. The tree is standing just inside a field, OS SJ 648767, adjacent to a cut-leaved beech. Many red oak, *Quercus rubra*, and fewer scarlet oak, *Quercus coccinea*, have been planted throughout the county but most are comparatively young trees.

The Pear

John Wesley selected a pear tree to preach under in Mr Priestner's garden in Oldfield Brow in 1751 on his second visit to the Altrincham area [8] but the fate of this tree is not known.

The Hazel or Hassle pear, a small hardy north country variety, was extensively grown in the area around Acton Bridge and Crowton from the end of the 19th century. The Hazel Pear Inn by the railway is named after this tree. Pears were sent in by rail to Liverpool market in large quantities. A yellow dye can be extracted from the skins and twigs and it is reported that in the First World War produce from the area was used for dying khaki uniforms in Liverpool. Few trees are left for most of the orchards were grubbed up in the sixties and seventies and converted to housing.

Plane (*Platanus x hispanica*)

This is the London plane which is a hybrid between the Oriental and American plane. There are mature examples to be found in the county including one at Cholmondeley Castle but they are not very frequent. A plane was planted at Eccleston Church to mark the Coronation of King George VI in 1937 and it is now an attractive specimen 12.5m high with an equivalent crown spread, and a diameter of 40cm at 1.5m.

Strawberry Tree (*Arbutus species*)

The native tree *Arbutus unedo*, was growing in woodland at Lyme Park in 1465. Now it can be found in some collections and gardens but no particularly large or old specimens are known. There is however a very good mature specimen of *Arbutus menziesii*, a species of strawberry tree from the west coast of America, standing in Royden Park, OS SJ 243857, which is 14.5m in height and 120cm in diameter at 1.3m, the tree forking at about 1.5m into two large stems of 76cm and 55cm diameter. The crown spread of 19m is impressive with the branching showing the typical pink to red peeling bark of this tree.

Sweet Chestnut (*Castanea sativa*)

There are many massive old trees in parks and old estate woods but none possibly better situated than the chestnut at the top of Tower Hill, Cholmondeley Castle. When the gardens are open you can climb up the path behind the Tea Room to find the chestnut and the reward is a magnificent panoramic view of much of the county. There are notable trees at Combermere Abbey, Capesthorne Hall, and Tatton Park where a tree 24.4m in height and 194cm in diameter at 1.5m was measured.

At Delamere in the hardwood belt on the side of the road leading from

27. Looking out from the sweet chestnut on Tower Hill, Cholmondeley Castle.

Hatchmere to Ashton there are many large old sweet chestnuts which were planted around 1820. Look for the spiral ridging on the bark and the nuts in season if the squirrels have not got there first.

A sweet chestnut at Alderley Park opposite the Tenants Hall is said to have been planted by Winston Churchill early in his political career, and is known as the Churchill Tree.

The Sycamore (*Acer pseudoplatanus*)

The twelve apostles were planted in a line along the boundary of glebe land at Malpas by a public footpath, OS SJ 483475. There are four large old trees remaining with nine younger trees planted as replacements for past losses. The largest is 187cm in diameter at 1.5m. The trees make a fine landscape feature, but why and when they were planted remains a mystery, though it is estimated that they go back to the second half of the 18th century.

Another magnificent sycamore of equivalent size is situated by the entrance to Henbury Hall, near Macclesfield, OS SJ 875731. A smaller, younger but beautifully shaped tree stands on the green at Astbury, an attractive setting with the church in the background.

The Tulip Tree (*Liriodendron tulipifera*)

One of the best examples of this tree is to be found on Arley Green, OS SJ 602808. The tree is around 150 years in age, with a height of 18.3m and a diameter of 107cm at 1.5m. The crown is 19m in width and the tree stands in a comparatively exposed situation. There is a cavity in the bole but careful tree surgery in the last twenty years had maintained the crown in good condition. What is particularly good to see is the replacement tulip tree already planted a few metres away, so that when the life of the grand old one finally ends there is a good sized youngster to take its place.

The lobed and truncated leaves of this tree have a curious look for they appear as if they have been snipped off with a pair of scissors.

Visitors to the Cholmondeley Castle Gardens can find a variegated form, *Auromarginata*, but it is still quite a small tree.

28. Typical spiralling bark of this sweet chestnut at Capesthorne.

Cedars

There are many fine mature cedars to be found on the Cheshire estates, but pride of place must go to the cedar of Lebanon, *Cedrus libani*, on the Eaton Estate which the Air Ministry wanted to fell in 1942 when the wartime runway was built. Instead it was decapitated at around 40 feet and served as a landmark for returning aircrews. Now fifty years on, it is a handsome heavily crowned tree of considerable though as yet unmeasured dimensions, in excellent health.

A much younger and smaller tree is the Deodar cedar, *Cedrus deodara*, planted by the Duke of Windsor in 1926 outside Windsor Hall at Reaseheath College. It has not grown particularly well on this site and contrasts with the very healthy luxuriant growth of the *Cedrus brevifolia* by the lake.

Cryptomeria

It is sometimes called the Japanese Red Cedar though it is not of the cedar family. There is a small mixed stand of maturing ornamental trees immediately to the west of Capesthorne Hall which includes Wellingtonia and some very well formed *Cryptomeria japonica*. The largest of the *Cryptomeria* has a height of 20m and a diameter of 79cm at 1.5m.

The Monkey Puzzle (*Araucaria araucana*)

This was a fashionable tree to plant in Victorian times. The largest tree to date found in Cheshire is growing in the Wilderness on the Adlington Estate. The typical straight cylindrical bole has a diameter of 70cm at 1.5m, while the tree height is 21m.

The Redwoods

The coast redwood, *Sequoia sempervirens*, is native to the American west coast where one of the trees is the world's tallest, over 110m (360') high. Examples in Cheshire are few and far between and all are comparatively small and young trees. Some were badly frosted in the severe winter of 1982 but recovered.

In the park at Eaton there is a small grove of eight trees which were presented to the 4th Duke of Westminster in 1966 by Mrs Thomas Naylor. They had been raised from seed from the renowned stand of redwoods at Leighton, near Welshpool. Now they are approximately 9.5m high and look very promising.

The dawn redwood, *Metasequoia glyptostroboides*, is a deciduous conifer which was only discovered in southwest China in 1941 and first introduced into this country in 1948. Examples can be found in most parks and there is a particularly fine specimen at Chester Zoo close to the south east corner which is already 18m high and 52cm in diameter at 1.5m. This tree is said to be only 25 years old.

The Wellingtonia, *Sequoiadendron giganteum*, is well represented in the county with many fine specimens. This species proved one of the most stormfirm in the gales which devastated many trees in the parks and woodlands in the south of England in October 1987 and later. A tree in the Cholmondeley Castle gardens is 178cm in diameter at 1.5m with a height of 36.3m (119').

The Swamp Cypress (*Taxodium distichum*)

This is a deciduous conifer very similar in appearance to the dawn redwood, but it has a much more rounded crown when mature while its leaves are alternate instead of opposite. Specimens are to be found on most of the estates, and in the Victorian parks. There is an outstanding example of this attractive tree in the garden at Dunham Massey close to the north east corner of the hall, where it is an ideal compliment to the building and softens rather a hard line.

The Yews

The evergreen yew was said to be symbolic of everlasting life in druid times. It has been planted by clergy in churchyards since the Norman Conquest, but some remaining trees predate this period for the tree can live on for centuries after the main bole has hollowed out with decay and the remaining outer bole has fragmented into sections, each with live branching.

According to Vaughan Cornish, planting positions are significant. At least two trees were planted, one by the path which leads from the funeral gateway of the churchyard to the principal entrance of the church, the other beside the path which leads to a second or lesser doorway [9].

Undoubtedly many old yews have been lost when churches have been enlarged and some have probably been felled as they were thought to be dangerous or dying. Fortunately Cheshire still has some extremely ancient churchyard yews and notable specimens can be found at:-

Astbury, St Mary - this is possibly the oldest yew in the county. Long ago the bole became hollow and all that remains are leaning sections of the outer bole propped up over the pathway, but there is considerable live branching and the tree should live for many more years. It is impossible to put an accurate date on this very ancient tree without carbon dating, but it is surely well over 1,000 years.

Eastham, St Mary - this fine old yew lives on but whether it is the tree that the villagers entreated the Abbot and monks of St Werburgh 'to have a care of ye olde yew' in 1152 when they received the manor of Eastham at the hands of Earl Randall of Chester, is not absolutely certain. The tree capsized years ago and only half a hollow trunk remains, yet from a distance the well-furnished rounded dark-green crown gives no indication that the tree has struggled to survive. It is thought that the tree pre-dated the Norman Conquest, the site being close to the east end of a timber-

29. One of the fine *Cryptomeria japonica* at Capesthorne.

30. Wellingtonia in Cholmondeley Castle Gardens.

framed wattle and daub chapel. It is probably more than 1,000 years old, but not quite the age of the Astbury yew.

Gawsworth, St James - There are four well-furnished yews typically sited at the corners of the churchyard, three of which are old trees almost certainly exceeding 500 years, though they are not particularly large. 400 years ago the churchyard wall was built round the largest of these trees which now has a diameter of 136cm at 1.5m.

Goostrey, St Lukes - there is a magnificent old yew standing close to the main door, which is a male tree with a hollow bole 255cm in diameter at 1m. This is the largest in the county, and despite the hollow trunk the foliage is luxuriant. Its age is probably over 1,000 years, but it does not appear to be as old as the Astbury yew.

Mobberley, St Wilfred - this most picturesque of churchyard yews is not a very old tree, possibly 500 years or more, but it is perfectly shaped and often used as a setting for wedding photographs. The tree has a height of 12.2m, crown spread of 14m and a diameter of 107cm at 1.5m.

Every effort should be made to retain these ancient churchyard yews which can live on and on with the minimum of attention. If any treatment is thought necessary, professional advice should first be obtained from qualified foresters or arboriculturists who have worked with old yews.

It is always difficult to assess the age of old trees. Size can be misleading for rates of growth vary with soil and site quality, and the conditions in which the tree is growing. For instance an oak 150 years old growing on good ground in forest conditions could have a diameter of 66cm yet on poor ground it could be only 46cm. Leading dendrologist, Alan Mitchell, has a rule of thumb for trees in the open that there is one inch of girth at 1.5m for every year of age, and for trees in a woodland half an inch per year. This was found to work quite well for maiden trees of several species in middle age [10]. Approximate ages given in this text are based on judgement and experience gained as a forester, and any circumstantial evidence. There has always been a tendency to overestimate the age of trees. Dryden wrote admiringly of the oak in the 17th century:-

> The monarch oak, the patriarch of trees,
> Shoots rising up and spreads by slow degrees;
> Three centuries he grows, and three he stays,
> Supreme in state, and in three more decays.

If he had used two century periods instead of three he would have been closer to reality, but his lines reflect the history and character of the ancient oaks remaining in Cheshire.

CHAPTER 13 - Hedgerows

Hedgerows in medieval times were much wider than those of today. Commoners were very tenacious of their rights of hedgebote for they obtained wood for faggots and hurdles, and branches and foliage for feeding livestock which were everyday necessities[1]. Ancient fences were described by Mr Fenna of Blackhurst as being composed of hazel, alder, white or blackthorn, wych elm, holly, dogwood, birch, and others [2]. Hedges have been planted from time immemorial to protect stock, crops, and farmsteads, while others are derived from a woodland edge.

The number of different species in a hedge gives some indication of its age. Hooper suggested age X could be estimated by counting the number of shrub species Y in a 30 yard stretch when X = 100Y +30 years. Hence there were just over 100 years for every species found [3]. However, a hedge could be derived from woodland when traces of woodland ground flora should be looked for, or it could be one in which several species were planted, so Hooper's Rule should be used with caution.

In his discourse on forest trees John Evelyn in 1662 recommended planting holly with the quicks - 'Let every fifth or sixth be a holly set'. After he had discussed the damage cattle could cause to plantations he concluded - 'Let us therefore shut up what we have thus laboriously planted, with some good quickset hedge'. He suggested adding at equal spaces of twenty or thirty feet a young oak or elm sucker, ash or the like which will come in time, or during early hedge establishment and maintenance sprinkling in some trees such as oak, ash, beech, maple, fruit and the like among the quicks.

The pattern of enclosure in Cheshire was generally achieved with the consent of all sections of the community. The majority of open fields were enclosed over the period 1600-1800, but commons, waste and mosses were mainly enclosed by Act of Parliament between 1750 and 1850 [4]. Many hedgerows were established during this period.

On many farm leases tree planting was specified as a condition. A High Legh estate lease dated 1740 has the following clause:- 'Shall and will yearly and every year during the said term, plant five young plants of oak, ash, poplar or elm, in convenient places in the hedges at convenient distances from one another upon the said premises, and shall and will use his and their best endeavors to preserve the same from destruction, and when and so often as any of he said plants shall happen to die, be broken, or destroyed, shall and will make up the deficiency by replanting the like number and sorts of young plants in the room or place of such of them as shall happen to die, be broken or destroyed'. This farm was 15 statute acres and the lease remained in force from 1740-1838 [5].

There were 97 leases for lives on the Derby Estate in Macclesfield Forest Township in 1820 and in all the lessees were obliged to plant trees [6]. Tenants on the Crewe lands had to plant trees each year, for example in a lease from John Crewe to Robert Parkin who had to both maintain a 1/4 acre plantation and plant five trees each year, and pay a 3/6d fine per tree if he failed to do so [7]. An indenture and lease dated 1774 by Thomas Massie of Coddington to George Dutton, Yeoman, cites the same four species of tree to be planted as those at High Legh:- oak, ash, poplar, or elm.

These were the four most important trees on estates and farms. Oak was much in demand for timber-framed houses, quality furniture, and shipbuilding, gates, spokes, postwood, cleft fencing and fuel. Ash was used for shafts, wheels, bentware, tool handles, carts, rails, while its firewood was superior to oak. Poplar was widely used for flooring in farm buildings, low grade furniture, boarding in carts and boxes. Elm was valuable for shipbuilding, for use underwater, wooden pipes, chairs, wheelwrights timber, and coffins. The four species of tree could meet most timber needs.

Many writers were very critical about the state of Cheshire hedgerows. In the Wirral they were described as exceedingly badly maintained and not fulfilling the purpose for which they were designed. Many were high and allowed to run wild covering two to three yards either side of the ditch, often preventing the circulation of air in small fields. Some farmers scarcely think it necessary to cut hedges [8].

In William Palin's Report on Cheshire Farming in 1843, he stated that fences were sadly neglected in many parts of the county, while if thorns are needed to repair a gap the work was performed carelessly [9]. Describing the Great Budworth area he said that there was much hedgerow timber sadly neglected. The 1792 Report by the Chairman of Chester Quarter Sessions said that the growth of oak timber in hedgerows was not much encouraged in the county [10].

At the end of the 19th century there was a body of opinion that did not approve of hedgerow trees. Thomas Conway, Forester at High Legh, wrote in a prize winning essay in 1899, that forest trees should never be planted in the line of thorns, for it was impossible even with the greatest care, to rear thorn plants to become a good and beautiful fence under their drip. He suggested that the reason why hedgerow timber was grown because it was the best way of growing timber for the navy and gives shelter to fields [11]. His comment about a tenanted farm on High Legh Estate which had had to plant hedgerow trees was 'Happily now this farm has no trees in its fences', and if his opinions had been accepted by Cheshire farmers across the county, hedgerow tree planting went out of fashion at about the turn of the century.

At that time Conway gave the cost of hedge planting per 100 yards as:-

800 Quicks @ 25/- per 1000	£1 0s 0d
Planting same	4s 0d
	£1 4s 0d

Hedgerow trees in Cheshire are a notable feature of the landscape and often give it an almost wooded appearance. By far the most frequent tree is the oak, but many other species occur. The Forestry Commission census of trees in the county in 1979-82 found that among non woodland trees occurring as isolated trees or linear features 36.1% were oak, 21.3% sycamore, 15.3% ash, and 27.3% other species [12]. Unfortunately almost all the elm were destroyed by Dutch Elm disease during the decade leading up to the census, though the elm was never as prominent in Cheshire as in some midland and southern counties. The census recorded 15,220 dead elms of over 7cm diameter at breast height out of a total of 18,910 live and dead elm trees.

Many of the isolated trees in fields were once part of hedgerows which have been removed. Unfortunately a previous Forestry Commission census in 1965-7, and the 1955 census of hedgerow and park timber, did not give separate figures for counties, so losses cannot be compared over the years 1955 to 1979-82. However Mark Rogers in a research project on certain Cheshire hedgerows [13] found that losses of hedgerow trees since 1947 on the Cheshire plains had been comparatively small, probably under 10%, with the major loss occurring in the period 1881-1947. He was able to use the 1st edition ordnance survey 6 inch maps for comparison purposes because they depicted individual trees, and his groundwork showed that existing mature oak corresponded to tree positions on the maps. The linear density of hedgerow trees had fallen from 58 trees per kilometre in 1881 to 25 in 1985, while during the same period hedgerow loss was 23%.

Was this loss due to new ideas on hedgerow management such as Thomas Conway was advocating in 1899, or was it caused by felling in the wars or felling to raise income in times of depression with no replacement planting? Most likely it was a combination of these factors.

In 1955, a committee chaired by Lord Merthyr looked into the extent to which the growth of hedgerow timber was compatible with good agricultural practice, and recommended the measures that should be taken to promote the growing and tending of hedgerow and farm timber wherever it could be done without harm to farm production [14]. The committee recommended that broadleaved trees which could be expected to yield the best hardwood timber should be grown where there is no reason to prefer other species; but full advantage should be taken of natural regeneration, and of opportunities for growing hybrid poplars, larch, chestnut coppice and willows in suitable places.

Many of our hedgerow trees are mature and showing signs of stress and die back. Old age takes its toll of trees but it does not explain the general decline in health that has been evident in the last two decades, and clear reasons for this are still sought. Trees have been affected by industrial pollution in the past. Land drainage and lowering of the water table, and some very dry summers have also been factors. Research is being carried out nationally to determine present pollution factors, and the effects of acid rain and climate on tree health.

The conservation value of well-managed and maintained hedgerows and hedgerow trees on the farm is immeasurable. In the long term saleable timber can be produced but there always need to be younger trees coming on to replace any fellings, so some planting together with care of self-sown trees is consistently required. What better than to plant our native species such as oak and ash, which also produce good timber and fit naturally into the landscape. The occasional overmature tree with holes and decay can be left standing as a habitat for insect fauna and other wildlife. Many an owl has a hollow tree as an abode.

Hedgerow maintenance is almost entirely carried out with tractor mounted mechanical trimmers, when it is only too easy to cut off any emerging tree saplings unless they are clearly marked or tagged before cutting. The craft of hedgelaying, necessary every twenty years or so to encourage new growth from the hedge stools and thicken the base, was almost lost but it has been steadily revived in the last few years. In laying, old hedge stems are almost severed at the base and bent over to make a barrier, held in place by small hedging stakes driven in between them and tied together with rods of pliable willow or hazel. The latter were formerly known as edders or eddrings, and the tying up known as eddering. The stools regenerate and a renewed dense strong stockproof base is formed.

Grants are available for hedge laying and gapping, and sometimes for the establishment of new hedgerows which can incorporate tree planting. The Hedgerow Incentive Scheme recently announced by the Countryside Commission will encourage the restoration and management of neglected and damaged hedgerows, priority going to those considered to be the most important environmentally. Advice on farm hedgerow and tree management can be obtained from the Farming and Wildlife Advisory Group Officer based at Reaseheath College, ADAS offices, or the Cheshire Landscape Trust.

CHAPTER 14 - The Present Situation and Future Hopes

There have only been minor changes in woodland area since the Forestry Commission censuś was completed ten years ago. This showed that there were 8,842 hectares of woodland or 3.8% of the area of Cheshire, well below the national average which is now approximately 10%. Being primarily an agricultural county there was not much scope for any extensive new planting until farmers were encouraged to diversify because of the agricultural surpluses. The Farm Woodlands Scheme was announced in 1988 but uptake was slow because the scheme terms were not sufficiently attractive. However the Farm Woodlands Premium Scheme which was introduced in 1992 offers increased incentives, and it is hoped more woodlands will be established. Demonstration plots can be seen at Reaseheath College.

There is also the opportunity to establish woodlands on areas of derelict land, waste ground, tip sites, and old mineral workings, for the experience and technology for dealing with such sites is increasingly available, together with grant assistance for carrying it out. There are still many such areas throughout the county which could be used for growing trees.

The Forestry Commission census[1] showed that woodlands were made up as follows, areas stated in hectares:-

Type of Woodland	State	Private or Other		Total
		Managed	Unmanaged	
Mainly conifer (over50%)	829	764	717	2310
Mainly broadleaf (over 50%)	73	775	5481	6329
Total High Forest (all ages)	902	1539	6198	8639
Coppice with standards		13		13
Coppice Woodland				
Scrub	1	36	75	112
Cleared Woodland	13	32	33	78
Grand Total	916	1620	6306	8842

The coppice with standards was classified as 5 hectares of ash and 8 hectares of chestnut coppice under oak standards, but it is understood that this area has since been converted into high forest. Over 17.5% or 959 hectares of the unmanaged mainly broadleaved woodland was considered to be of coppice origin, confirming that coppices used to be much more extensive. Woodland managed as coppice, with part being cut every year on a rotational basis so that there are always areas of different size and age in the wood, is particularly favourable for nature conservation for there is a continuous range of habitats, though they are rotating within the wood.

The problem with maintaining coppice woodland is the high cost, for the work in cutting and converting produce is labour intensive and requires considerable skills, and the small diameter poles, rods, and brushwood produced are difficult to market in quantity. There could be the opportunity for re-establishing coppices on a limited scale if production could be linked to a particular industry, such as supporting a charcoal production unit. This was often their function in the 16th and 17th centuries when coppices met the firewood needs of the salt industry and the charcoal needs of the ironmasters. There is the possibility that woodchips from fastgrown coppice could be used as the fuel for small power generating schemes.

History shows that woodlands whose produce has met particular needs, have been managed, cut, and regenerated on a sustained basis and have survived in the long term. It was when woods had fallen out of production that neglect had set in, and pressures arose to convert woodland to farmland or some other land use. Much the same arguments apply today. Woods need to be positively managed and used with timber being harvested at the appropriate time, or they will deteriorate and fall into neglect.

The area of unmanaged woodland shown in the census was over 70% of the total, and this is cause for considerable concern as these woodlands need to be conserved in order to obtain full benefit from them in the future.

Trees and the Environment

The environmental benefits of trees and woodlands are extremely important to us. Much is heard of the greenhouse gases whose concentrations are increasing worldwide and are likely to continue to do so probably resulting in a warmer Britain in years to come. Fortunately our main tree species should grow satisfactorily in a warmer climate provide rainfall is at least maintained, while if it increases growth rates may improve.

Tree canopies filter out pollutants and particles from the atmosphere and generally perform a very useful function in this respect, though there could be disadvantages if leaf and needle-fall transfers any collected pollutants into water courses. More importantly, vigorous growing trees help to reduce the carbon dioxide concentrations and lock up carbon in their timber for a considerable period.

The faster a tree grows the faster it is locking away carbon, so species like Corsican pine and the hybrid poplars which produce large volumes of timber quickly are doing more for us in this respect than the oak and slower growing hardwoods. The oak, ash, and other native hardwoods have much more to contribute to the environment in other respects, particularly in connection with the maintenance of our native wildlife, flora, and landscape, so a wide range of species is desirable.

New planting provides the opportunity for creating different habitats for wildlife and extending existing ones. Eyesores and industrial sites can be screened. Derelict land and mineral workings can be restored to woodland, which if sensitively designed can make a significant contribution to the landscape. If these areas can be linked up by green corridors, the public have access to them for recreational purposes, and some existing woodland areas are added in, the concept of the community forest emerges.

The Mersey Forest

The proposal for a community forest now known as the Mersey Forest was approved by Government in February 1991, when funding for a Core Team to plan and initiate the forest was announced. The team is based at Risley Moss which is

31. The location of the Mersey Forest.

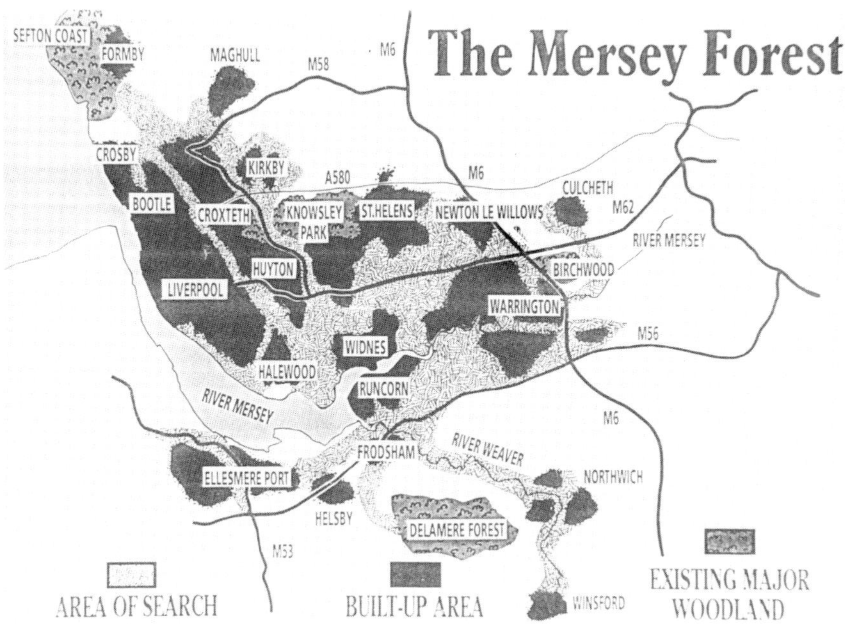

central to the proposed forest which covers parts of four authorities in Cheshire:- Warrington, Halton, Vale Royal, and Ellesmere Port and Neston Borough Councils together with four adjacent authorities in Merseyside. It is hoped to supplement areas of existing woodland by planting up to 200 hectares a year for 10 to 15 years to create a 7,500 hectare forest. The first plantings in Cheshire took place last season on an area close to the Anderton Boat Lift near Northwich and at Clincton Wood, Widnes. The areas within which it is hoped to create the woodland blocks to make up the forest are shown on the map.

It is envisaged that the forest will ultimately consist of a network of woodlands linked by walking, cycling, and riding trails. It will be a multi-purpose forest with the objectives of improving the landscape, providing recreational and educational facilities, producing timber to meet national needs and help finance the forest in the long term, and creating new wildlife habitats, corridors, and shelter. There will be different priorities to suit particular needs. In some woods landscape might be given priority in a combination of several objectives, in other parts nature conservation, timber production, or a form of recreation could be given first priority. There will be the opportunity for community involvement in shaping the future forest, and participating in planting and maintaining it.

This is a very exciting prospect but it cannot be fulfilled without the support of those who own and manage the land, be they individuals, authorities, corporate bodies, or industries, together with adequate fiscal incentives to get the scheme off the ground and a stable long term commitment from central government of whatever party.

Forest Products and Industries

Periodic thinning is necessary in woodlands both to give trees more space as they grow to maturity, and to maintain woodland hygiene. Timber trees are harvested at maturity and it is the sale of this timber and the larger thinnings that finances woodland management and maintenance. There is a cost if mature trees are not felled before they start to decline in their old age, so any benefits from retaining them must outweigh this and there will be cases where they do. It is good to keep a few overmature trees, for their decaying and deadwood sustains a wide range of invertebrate and other wildlife.

Markets for produce and efficient marketing are two essentials for any viable woodland enterprise. Though Cheshire has no large wood industry or major sawmill using home grown timber within its borders, it is very well placed regionally. There are two large industries situated just outside the county. The Shotton Paper Company produces newsprint using spruce and pine thinnings, softwood residues, and recycled newsprint and magazines. This provides a valuable outlet for spruce and pine thinnings from Cheshire woodlands. Not much spruce is grown in

Cheshire for the climate is not ideal, but pine grows well on the light soils where quality hardwoods can not be produced, and is particularly useful on reclamation sites. The Kronospan Group at Chirk manufactures chipboard, both melamine faced boards and flooring grades using softwood, most hardwoods except oak, and sawmill residues (waste) in the process. This provides an outlet for both hardwood and softwood thinnings, though oak is excluded. In addition there is a series of large modern sawmills straddling the Welsh Marches, within reasonable haulage distance of the county, providing markets for timber sized hardwood and softwood logs. There are smaller outlets within the county which mainly take in softwood material for making up fencing panels and pallets.

Industry primarily demands softwood and generally there is little difficulty in marketing it from small diameter material up to large sawlogs. There is a ready market for quality hardwood sawlogs, such as oak, beech, ash, and sycamore, but it is difficult finding outlets for the lower timber grades and hardwood thinnings. Those that there are provide little return, and sometimes a loss in the case of thinnings when harvesting costs are taken into account.

The demand for wood is expected to go on rising certainly well into the 21st century. In 1991 the United Kingdom imported timber based products to the value of £6,342 million and exported £1,807 million, a trade deficit in timber based products of £4,535 million out of a total trade deficit of £14,053 million. Wood accounted for over 32% of our trade deficit[2]. The United Kingdom must grow more timber, and if more quality hardwoods can be grown to reduce hardwood imports it would also help to ease pressure on the rainforests.

More broadleaved planting is being carried out but there is need to find new outlets and uses for hardwood thinnings, and need to concentrate on producing quality sawlogs. The latter would involve planting at closer espacement than the currently accepted 3 x 3 metres or interplanting nurse species. Oak, ash, sycamore, beech, and cherry are the hardwoods most in demand. Softwoods will continue to be grown to meet the bulk of industrial needs, but in Cheshire they will mainly be grown in mixture with hardwoods or as nurses for them. The great destructive threat of the grey squirrel to pole sized hardwoods and some conifers remains and control measures need to be taken by all landowners if the population is to be kept at a low level and damage is to be minimised.

Trees and the Landscape

Trees are such a vital and well loved feature of the Cheshire landscape that it is fortunate that the landscape appearance of woodlands can usually be maintained when the time comes to fell timber and replant, by retaining parts of the fringe and groups of trees which also help to shelter the young crop.

In town and open countryside trees have to be replaced when they are overmature or dangerous, though safe life can often be extended by judicious tree surgery which is particularly worthwhile if trees are of considerable historical or landscape importance. Conversely, careless tree surgery can do untold damage, so it is always worth checking with your Council forestry staff to see if they maintain a list of approved contractors before ordering any work. Tree surgery also buys time to plant future replacements well before they are needed. Cheshire is fortunate for Reaseheath College provides training courses in arboriculture to professional diploma standard. The care and maintenance of our young tree stock as well as our older trees is one of the concerns of the Cheshire Landscape Trust. Many trees continue to be lost through neglect and carelessness, while on building sites older trees are damaged because of insufficient protection. Often young trees are disregarded on these sites, yet they are our future landscape. Horses and ponies in a paddock will almost certainly remove the bark from any large unprotected trees. Young trees also need protecting against browsing livestock and rabbits by appropriate fencing and tree guards. Tree ties need to be loosened off as trees grow to avoid strangulation, and weeding is necessary in the first few years after planting. A little care and attention at the right time is all that is needed to give the trees a good start. We need them, and more.

The Cheshire Landscape Trust runs a Tree Warden scheme in the county to help communities be more tree conscious, keep an eye on trees in the neighbourhood, and encourage planting, care, and maintenance. There are already 68 Parishes with wardens, some have two. The wardens are doing a valuable job which future generations will appreciate all the more. It is hoped that the whole county can be covered in this way.

The Forest Authority

In 1992 the Forestry Commission divided into the Forest Enterprise which manages and runs the state forests such as Delamere, and the Forest Authority which implements Government forest policy and legislation, a change generally welcomed by foresters. It is the Forest Authority who issue and supervise felling licences, agree woodland grant schemes, and pay grants. The Authority is also responsible for the research advisory service and plant health requirements. The latter includes the issue of licences required to move spruce logs coming out of Cheshire woods, a measure to help control the spread of the Great Spruce Bark Beetle, and checking of imported timber and beetle traps baited at the docks to catch new unwanted species coming in to the country.

Authority Woodland Officers who cover Cheshire and the Merseyside and Greater Manchester areas are based at Delamere, Tel: 0606 889912. They should be contacted concerning any woodland matters, grant and felling licence applications.

They liaise closely with County and District Councils whose forestry staffs can also be contacted for help and advice. In the case of any work required on trees covered by Tree Preservation Orders or trees situated in Conservation Areas, application should be made to the Council whose permission must be obtained in writing before any work is carried out.

Woodlands to Visit

There is plenty of opportunity to get out into Cheshire woodlands. Delamere Forest and Macclesfield Forest are both managed as commercial forests yet provide wide opportunity for public recreation and enjoyment and at the same time provide quiet havens for wildlife. These are the areas to visit to get the feel of a working forest. There are always areas being felled, thinned, and planted so there is a range of age class and woodland conditions to see. There are many woodland areas in the county which are open to the public. The extensive National Trust woods on Alderley Edge are particularly attractive with mature mixed woodland of beech, pine, and oak, and some very striking viewpoints. The Sandstone Trail along the Peckforton Hills passes through areas of ancient semi-natural sessile oak woodland and mixed plantations, and then on to the heath vegetation which birch is invading at Maiden Castle, another great viewpoint. At Little Budworth Country Park there are considerable areas of birch and oak clad heathland, intermixed with glades and mire. Stanney Wood, close to Ellesmere Port, though its trees are comparatively young is an ancient semi-natural woodland. The oak is mainly of coppice or seedling origin from the time it was last felled probably about 50 years ago, and it has been continuously wooded for centuries. Marbury Country Park, close to Northwich, also contains areas of semi-natural ancient woodland as well as some interesting older conifer plantations, specimen trees, avenues, and parkland. Burton Wood on the Wirral is a National Trust property, not so extensive but containing mature mixed woodland. A visit there would combine nicely with one to Ness Gardens nearby. Much of Poynton Coppice is owned by the Macclesfield Borough Council and is open to the public with access from Shrigley Road and Middlewood Way. This old coppice was planted up to high forest in the 19th century and it was last felled in 1945. The flora is particularly rich. Not far away at Lyme Park, National Trust woods, avenues, and parkland with deer, can be visited. There are also deer parks at Tatton and Dunham Massey, both National Trust properties, with woodlands containing magnificent old oak, beech, and lime. These are all easily accessible. There are others, while many more woodlands can be reached by public footpaths which pass through them or alongside but do respect private property.

In conclusion an admirable summary of objectives for woodlands in Cheshire is given in *A Woodland Strategy For Cheshire* published in January 1992 [3].

Cheshire's woodlands are a viable and renewable natural resource, capable of providing a continuous supply of raw material in the form of timber and timber products, along with visual amenity, habitats for wildlife and nature conservation, opportunities for farm diversification, peaceful recreational pursuits and the study of many aspects of natural and rural history.

Woodlands cannot be conserved without management, which is almost always a compromise that balances out the different objectives. The forester is at the hub of things putting the management plan into practice and maintaining and working the wood to the best of his ability. He is able to obtain advice on particular problems from a wide range of agencies, and he welcomes informed criticism. He is usually worth listening to and deserving of support for he has the long term future of the wood at heart. After all it was the forester of yesteryear, guided and supported by the landowners of the day, who nurtured the wonderful mixed woods in Cheshire that we enjoy and reap the benefits of today.

There is a wealth of experience from the past to add to the new techniques and skills continually being acquired. These are encompassed in the high standards of forestry training set by the industry which augers well for the future.

REFERENCES

Chapter 1 - The Landscape Background

Chapter 2 - The Ancient Woodland

1 Linnard W B, 1982, *Welsh Woods & Forests*, National Museum Of Wales, p4
2 Ibid, p5.
3 Rackham O, 1990, *Trees & Woodland in the British Landscape*, J M Dent & Sons, p35.
4 Lady Newton ,1917, *House of Lyme*, William Heinemann, p10.
5 Mitchell A F, *Native British Trees*, Forestry Commission Research Information Note 53.80.SILS.
6 Tansley A G, 1939, *British Isles & their Vegetation*, Cambridge University Press, p294.
7 Rackham O, 1990, *Trees & Woodland in the British Landscape*, J M Dent & Sons, p114 - 6.
8 Ibid, p125 - 6.
9 Peterken G F, 1981, *Woodland Conservation and Management*, Chapman & Hall, p17.
10 Newton A, 1971, *Flora of Cheshire*, Cheshire Community Council, p154.
11 Robinson D P & Whitbread A, 1988, *Cheshire Inventory of Ancient Woodlands*, Nature Conservancy Council, p10.

Chapter 3 - Sources of Historical Information on Woodland

1 Chambers F M, Lageard J, Thomas P A, 1992, *Pollen and Tree Ring Studies, White Moss Alsager*, Cheshire Past, Issue 1, p4.
2 Howard-Davies C, Stocks C, Innes J, 1988, *Peat & the Past*, Lancaster University Press, p24.
3 Morris J, 1978, *Domesday Book 26 Cheshire*, Phillimore 1.26, 9.13.
4 Rackham O, 1986, *The History of the Countryside*, J M Dent & Sons, p78.
5 Morris J, 1978, *Domesday Book 26 Cheshire*, Phillimore 1.10, 1.1.
6 *Lands at Appleton 1760* and *Lands at Sutton 1754 Maps*, Archives at Arley Hall.
7 Cheshire CRO, DCH PP2.
8 Survey Of Cheshire Estates Of Sir B Broughton-Delves In Parishes Of Wybunbury, Audlem, & Acton 1762, Private Collection.

Chapter 4 - Early Woodland Management

1 Mitchell A F, *The Native and Exotic Trees in Britain*, DOE Arboriculture Research Note 29.81.SILS, pp1 - 3.
2 Hampshire Countryside Heritage, 1983, *Ancient Woodland*, p10.
3 Peterken G F, 1981, *Woodland Conservation & Management*, Chapman & Hall, p20.
4 Rackham O, 1991, *Trees and Woodland in the British Landscape*, J M Dent & Sons, p67.
5 Ibid, p22.
6 Earwaker J P, 1877, *History of East Cheshire*, Vol 2, p292.
7 James N D G, 1981, *History of British Forestry*, Blackwell, pp125 - 6.
8 Chetham Society ,1876, *Ancient Parish of Prestbury*, Vol XCVII, p202.
9 Lasdun S, 1991, *The English Park*, Andre Deutsch, p7, p13.
10 Letters & Accounts of William Brereton of Malpas, Record Society of Lancashire & Cheshire,Vol CXVI, p51.
11 Mitchell A F, 1980, *Native British Trees*, Forestry Commission Research Information Note 53. 80. SILS, p3.

Chapter 5 - The Royal Forests

1 Linnard W B, 1982, *Welsh Woods and Forests*, National Museum of Wales, p23, p25.
2 *Victoria County History* (hereafter *VCH*), Vol II 1979, Oxford University Press, p172.
3 Ibid, p176.
4 Ibid, p178.
5 Ibid, p177.
6 Ibid, p176.
7 *Delamere, History of a Cheshire Parish*, 1991, Local History Group, p25.
8 Ibid, p44.
9 *VCH*, Vol II, 1979, Oxford University Press, p176.
10 Ibid, p176.
11 Ibid, p176.
12 Ibid, p178.

13 Ibid, p178.
14 Ibid, p179.
15 Ormerod G, 1882, *History of Cheshire*, Macclesfield Hundred, p282.
16 Morris J, *Domesday Book 26, Cheshire*, 1978, Phillimore, 1.25, 1.26.
17 Ormerod G, 1882, *History of Cheshire*, p280.
18 *VCH*, Vol II, 1979, Oxford University Press, p183.
19 Ibid, p183.
20 Ibid, p179.
21 Curry A, 1983, *The Court Rolls of Macclesfield 1345 - 1485*, Cheshire History No 12 Autumn, p6.
22 Ormerod G, 1882, *History of Cheshire, Macclesfield Hundred*, p282.
23 Davies C S, 1961, *History of Macclesfield*, University of Manchester Press, p44.
24 *VCH*, Vol II, 1979, Oxford University Press, p184.
25 Walter Smith, Forest & Clough Paper 52, 23.10.41, Macclesfield Reference Library.
26 *VCH*, Vol II, 1979, Oxford University Press, p184.
27 Ibid, p184.
28 Ibid, p187.
29 Ibid, p186.
30 Ibid, p186.
31 Ibid, pp186 - 7.
32 Williams Mortimer W, 1847, *History of the Hundred of the Wirral*, p158.

Chapter 6 - Early Wood Consuming Industries

1 Morris J,*Domesday Book 26 Cheshire*, 1978, Phillimore, S1, S2, S3.
2 G D Twigg Correspondence.
3 Ibid.
4 Morris J, *Domesday Book 26 Cheshire*, 1978, Phillimore, 8.31.
5 G D Twigg Correspondence.
6 *Two Medieval Salt Houses Excavated in Wood Street, Nantwich*, 1980, A Salt Museum Publication, Cheshire Libraries & Museums.
7 *VCH*, Vol II,1979, Oxford University Press, p178.
8 Record Society Lancashire & Cheshire, Vol 68, p44.
9 Hurst Vase R, 1977, *Glassmaking at Kingswood Delamere*, Winsford Local History Society.
10 Edlin J T, 1949, *Woodland Crafts in Great Britain*, Batsford, pp88 - 89.
11 Hodson J L, 1978, *Cheshire 1660 - 1760*, Cheshire Community Council, p138.
12 Ibid, p138.
13 Davies C S, 1960, *Agricultural History of Cheshire 1750 - 1850*, Chetham Society, p12.
14 Aikin J, 1795, *Description of the Country 30 - 40 Miles Around Manchester*, p48.
15 Cheshire CRO, DCH/C 662.
16 Edlin J T, 1949, *Woodland Crafts in Great Britain*, Batsford, p87.
17 Carlon C J, 1979, *Alderley Edge Mines*, John Sherratt & Son, p72.
18 Anon, 1842, *Alderley Edge and its Neighbourhood*, Swynnerton, p5 - 6.
19 Carlon C J, 1981, *Gallantry Bank Mine*, John Sherratt & Son, p28, p47.
20 Ibid, p28.
21 Hodson J L, 1978, *Cheshire 1660 - 1760*, Cheshire Community Council, p143.
22 Linnard W B, 1982, *Welsh Woods and Forests*, National Museum of Wales, p73.
23 Hodson J L, 1978, *Cheshire 1660 - 1760*, Cheshire Community Council, p143.
24 Beck J, 1969, *Tudor Cheshire*, Cheshire Community Council, p52.
25 Shercliff W, Kitching D, & Ryan J, 1983, *Poynton a Coal Mining Village*, p14.
26 Ibid, p6.
27 Stewart Brown R, 1932, *Liverpool Ships in the 18th Century*, Hodder & Stoughton.
28 Merseyside Maritime Records Centre LNRS 3/22/137, p109.
29 Cheshire CRO, LNW/1.
30 Cheshire CRO, MF 228/1.
31 Warburton Muniments, John Rylands University Library Manchester (hereafter JRULM), Accounts Vouchers 28.9.1759 - 29.4.1763.
32 Cheshire CRO, DDX 289.2.
33 James N D G, 1981, *History of British Forestry*, Blackwell, p160.

Chapter 7 - The Development of the Nursery Trade

1 Anon ,1842, *Alderley Edge and its Neighbourhood*, Swynnerton, p1.
2 Cheshire CRO, DCH/A243.
3 Harvey J, 1972, *Early Gardening Catalogues*, Phillimore, pp29 - 30.
4 Warburton Muniments, JRULM, Accounts Vouchers 27.8.1756.
5 Harvey J, 1972, *Early Gardening Catalogues*, Phillimore, pp26 - 28.
6 Linnard W B, 1982, *Welsh Woods & Forests*, National Museum of Wales, p105.
7 Warburton Muniments, JRULM, Accounts Vouchers 19.4.1755, 15.3.1758, 10.12.1764, 12.12.1764.
8 Dunham Home Farm Accounts Book, JRULM, 1774 - 91, Box 531.
9 Survey of Cheshire Estates of Sir B Broughton-Delves in Parishes of Wybunbury, Audlem & Acton 1762, Doddington, Private Collection.
10 Wood, *History of the RSA*, p145.
11 Warburton Muniments, JRULM, Accounts Vouchers 2.4.1761.
12 Harvey J, 1974, *Early Nurserymen*, Phillimore, pp112 - 3.
13 Ibid, pp110 - 11.
14 Ibid, pp111.
15 RSA Library, Agricultural Minutes 1800 - 1801 Ashton, RSA C10/60/F2 and C10/154/F2 Taxall
16 *Journal of English Aboricultural Society1899*, Vol III, pp163 - 7.
17 Hault J, Notes & Articles on Liverpool History, City of Liverpool Records Library.
18 Fourth Triennial Report of Commissioners Of His Majesty's Woods, Forests & Land Revenue 1823.
19 Dunham Massey Accession List Records, JRULM, Box 14.
20 RSA Library, Transactions, 1802.
21 Shercliff W, Kitching D, Ryan J, 1983, *Poynton a Coal Mining Village*, p6.
22 Capesthorne Estate Muniments, JRULM, Contract Note Books 1861 - 1901.
23 Caldwell S W, 1964, *Recollections of Caldwell Family*, Cheshire CRO DDX 363.30.
24 Cheshire CRO, DDX 363.
25 *Journal of English Arboricultural Society 1899*, Vol VI, p352.
26 Hale Civic Society, 1987, *Hale & Ashley the Past 100 Years*, p243.
27 Public Records Office, Kew, F/8/37.
28 Ibid, F/8/38.
29 Ibid, F/8/39.
30 Popert E H, 1908, *Delamere Report*, Forestry Commission Library Alice Holt 62d (410.46).

Chapter 8 - Forestry on the Cheshire Estates

1 Anon ,1842, *Alderley Edge and its Neighbourhood*, Swynnerton, p.1
2 Accession List Records, Ex Dunham Massey Hall, 12.9.78., JRULM, Box 15 .
3 Sir Peter Leicester's Chapel Register 1678.
4 Cheshire CRO, Arderne Papers, DAR D66.
5 Warburton Muniments, JRULM, 1699 Notebook.
6 Ibid, Accounts Vouchers 1758 - 70.
7 Cheshire CRO, Adams Weekly, MF228/1.
8 Chester RO, *Grosvenor Estate Account Books*, Robert Pigot and Robert Vigar 1738 - 56.
9 Ibid, Thomas Burton 1675 - 82.
10 Linnard W B, 1982, *Welsh Woods & Forests*, National Museum of Wales, p72.
11 *Dunham Massey Guide 1991*, The National Trust, p41.
12 Survey of Cheshire Estates of Sir B Broughton-Delves in Parishes of Wybunbury, Audlem & Acton 1762, Private Collection.
13 Wood, *History of the RSA*, p145.
14 Tatton Muniments, JRULM, Egerton Family Correspondence 2/1/41.
15 Warburton Muniments, JRULM, Accounts Vouchers 29.5.1760.
16 James N D G, 1981, *History of English Forestry*, Blackwell, p309.
17 Warburton Muniments, JRULM, Accounts Vouchers 6. 5. 1772.
18 Carlon C J, 1979, *Alderley Edge Mines*, John Sherratt, p14.
19 Cheshire CRO, DSA241/1 Farm Accounts.
20 Chester RO, Grosvenor Estate Account Books 11.4.1755.
21 Holland W B, 1808, *General View of the Agriculture of Cheshire*, p198.

22 Accession List Records Ex Dunham Massey Hall 12.9.78, JRULM, Box 15 *Windblown Trees Dunham Massey Park 1802.*

23 RSA Library, Agricultural Minutes 1801 - 2.

24 Ibid, C10/60/F2 and C10/154/F2.

25 Holland W B, 1808, *General View of the Agriculture of Cheshire*, p201..

26 Ormerod G, 1882, *History of Cheshire*, p381

27 Wood, *History of the RSA*, p149.

28 Ibid, p149.

29 11th Report of the Commissioners Enquiring into the State of the Woods & Forests of the Crown, 1792

30 Cheshire CRO, CDX 363/9.

31 Harvey J H, 1973, *Forest Trees & their Prices Before 1850*, Quarterly Journal of Forestry, Vol LXVII, pp28 - 31.

32 Accession List Ex Dunham Massey Hall 12.9.78, JRULM, Box 14 *Trees Planted & Acorns Set in Estates 1807.*

33 Mitchell A F, 1980, *Native British Trees*, Forestry Commission Information Note 53/80/SILS.

34 Capesthorne Estate Muniments, JRULM, Contract Work Books February 87, February 88.

35 Greenwood Col G, 1876, *The Tree Lifter*, Longmans Green p8 - 9.

36 Davies C S, 1960, *Agricultural History of Cheshire 1750 - 1850*, Chetham Society, p93.

37 RSA Transactions of Society, Vol XIV, 1796, p22.

38 Accession List Records Ex Dunham Massey Hall 12.9.78, JRULM, Box 15 *Windblown Trees in Dunham Massey Park 1802.*

39 Warburton Muniments, JRULM, Accounts Vouchers 1826.

40 *Lands at Sutton Map 1754,* Archives at Arley Hall.

41 Cheshire CRO, DCH/C 662.

42 Latham B, 1957, *Timber*, Harrap & Co, p209.

43 RSA Journal March 1992, The Dingley Brothers.

44 Select Committee, Crown Forests 1854 - 56.

45 *Sawmill and Pumphouse, Dunham Massey*, 1983 National Trust Publication.

46 Capesthorne Muniments, JRULM, Monthly Reports 1897 - 1900 and 1885 - 1893, John Shaw Report on Permanent Improvements.

47 *Quarterly Journal of Forestry*, Vol XXVI, 1932, p368.

48 *Journal of English Arboricultural Association 1899*, Vol III, p166 - 7.

49 Ibid, Vol IV 1900, p354.

50 Cheshire CRO, DTW2477/E/4.

51 James N D G ,1981, *History of English Forestry*, Blackwells, p221.

52 Cheshire CRO, DTW2477/E/4.

Chapter 9 - Delamere and Macclesfield Forests from the 19th Century Onwards

1 Holland W B, 1808, *General View of the Agriculture of Cheshire*, p201.

2 1st Report Commissioners of His Majesty's Woods & Forests 1812.

3 Simpson E S, 1967, *Reclamation of Royal Forest of Delamere Liverpool Essays in Geography*, Longmans, p270.

4 2nd Report Commissioners of His Majesty's Woods & Forests, 1816.

5 4th Report, Ibid, 1823.

6 5th Report, Ibid, 1826.

7 30th Report, Ibid, Appendix 12a, 1852.

8 Ibid, Appendix 12c.

9 Select Committee Crown Forests 1854, para 490 - 1.

10 Ibid, para 411.

11 Ibid, para 476.

12 Ibid, para 484.

13 Ibid, para 550.

14 Ibid, para 597.

15 !st Report Select Committee on Woods, Forests & Land Revenues of The Crown, 1849, p403, para 8210.

16 Select Committee Crown Forests 1854, para 592.

17 Ibid, para 541.

18 Ibid, para 602 - 5

19 Ibid, para 611.
20 Ibid, Appendix 3, p166.
21 Ibid, para 1704.
22 Ibid, Proceedings, para 2.
23 Ibid, Proceedings, para 13.
24 Simpson E S, 1967, *Reclamation of Royal Forest of Delamere Liverpool Essays in Geography*, Longmans, p285.
25 PRO Kew, F8/40 Clutton Report to Commissioners.
26 Head Forester Jones, c1930. *Delamere Forest History*.
27 Cheshire CRO, MF204/16, *Chester Chronicle* 26.3.1892.
28 PRO Kew, F8/37.
29 Ibid.
30 PRO Kew, F8/37.
31 Ibid.
32 PRO Kew, F8/38.
33 Ibid.
34 Ibid.
35 Popert E H, 1908, *Delamere Report*, Forestry Commission Library Alice Holt 62d (410.46).
36 *Journal of Forestry*, Vol IV, p328.
37 PRO Kew, F8/8.
38 Ibid.
39 James N D G, 1981, *History of English Forestry*, Blackwell, pp210 - 215.
40 Jones G W, 1930, *Sale of Conifer Thinnings*, Journal of Forestry Commission 9, pp32 - 34.
41 Popert E H, 1908, *Delamere Report*, Forestry Commission Library Alice Holt 902 (410.46), p3.
42 Ibid, para19.
43 Ibid, p8.
44 Popert E H, 1908, *Delamere Report*, Forestry Commission Library Alice Holt 902 (410.46), p20.
45 Ibid, p9.

Chapter 10 - The Victorian Parks

1 Lasdun S, 1991, *The English Park*, Andre Deutsch, pp149 - 151.
2 Ibid, p162.
3 Laurie I C, 1987, *East Cheshire Parks & Gardens*, Sigma Press, p144.

Chapter 11 - Arboreta and Tree Collections

Chapter 12 - Historic and Notable Trees

1 Scard G, 1981, *Squire & Tenant: Rural Life in Cheshire 1760 - 1900*, Cheshire Community Council, p4.
2 Hold C, 1976, *History of British Folk Customs*, Granada, p33.
3 Milne Redhead E, 1990, *BSBI Black Poplar Survey 1973 - 88*, Watsonia 18, pp1 - 2.
4 Turner R C, 1990, *Gawsworth Hall Gardens*, Macclesfield & Vale Royal Groundwork Trust, p19.
5 Aiken, 1795, *A Description of the Country From 30 - 40 Miles Round Manchester*, p48.
6 *Journal of Archaeological and Historic Society of Chester 1876*, p300.
7 Mee A, 1938, *Cheshire*, Hodder & Stoughton, p20.
8 Ingham A, 1879, *History of Altrincham and Bowden*, Mackie Brewtnall & Co, p130.
9 Vaughan Cornish, 1946, *The Churchyard Yew*, Frederick Muller, p27.
10 Rackham O, 1990, *Trees &Woodland in the British Landscape*, J M Dent & Son, p13.

Chapter 13 - Hedgerows

1 Beddall J L, 1940, *Hedges for Farm & Garden*, Faber & Faber, p37.
2 Holland, 1808, *General View of the Agriculture of Cheshire*, p121.
3 Dowdeswell W H, 1987, *Hedgerows & Verges*, Allan & Unwin, p30.
4 Scard G, 1981, *Squire & Tenant: Rural Life in Cheshire 1760 - 1900*, Cheshire Community Council, pp7 - 8.
5 *Journal of English Arboricultural Association 1899*, Vol VI, pp49 - 50.
6 Stella Davies C, 1960, *Agricultural History of Cheshire 1750 - 1850*, Chetham Society, pp39 - 40.
7 Scard G, 1981, Ibid 4, p40.
8 Williams Mortimer W, 18447, *History of The Hundred of the Wirral*, p147.

9 Palin W, 184 , *Cheshire Farming*, p45.
10 11th Report of the Commissioners Enquiring into the State and Condition of the Woods & Forests of the Crown 1792.
11 *Journal of English Arboricultural Society1899*, Vol VI.
12 *Cheshire Census of Woodlands &Trees 1979 - 82*, Forestry Commission.
13 Rogers M, 1989, *Unpublished Open University Changing Countryside Project*, 3.4, p10.
14 *Report of the Committee on Hedgerow & Farm Timber*, HMSO 1955, pp53 -4.

Chapter 14 - The Present Situation and Future Hopes

1 Cheshire, Census of Woodlands & Trees 1979 - 82 Forestry Commission Table 2, p9.
2 *The Forestry Industry Year Book 1991 - 2*, Forestry Industry Committee of Great Britain, p20.
3 A Woodland Strategy For Cheshire 1992, Environmental Planning Service, Cheshire County Council, p19.

INDEX

CHESHIRE ESTATES

TREES

CHESHIRE WOODS AND FORESTS

PEOPLE